CW01510921

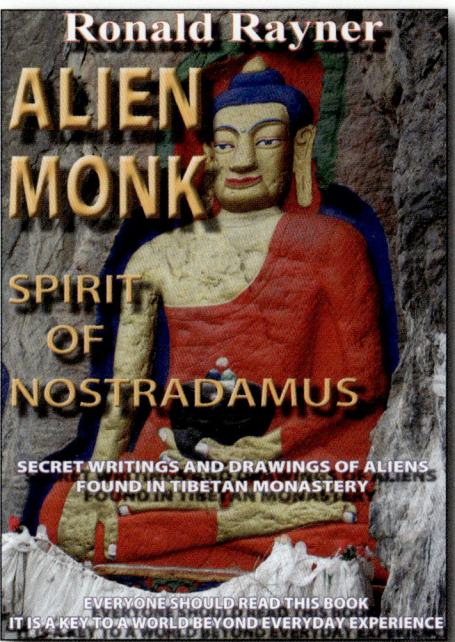

Amazon Books

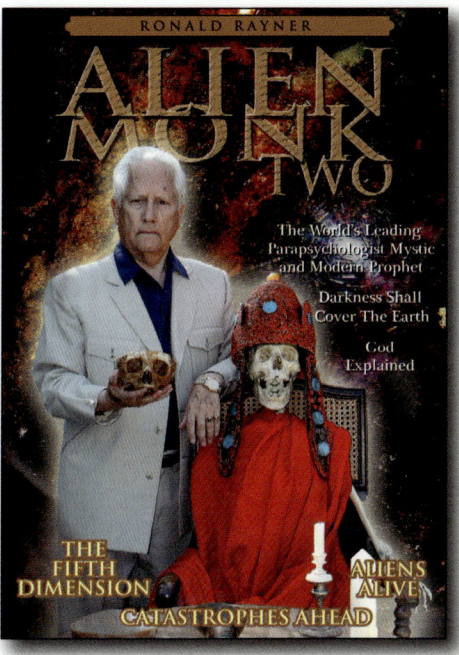

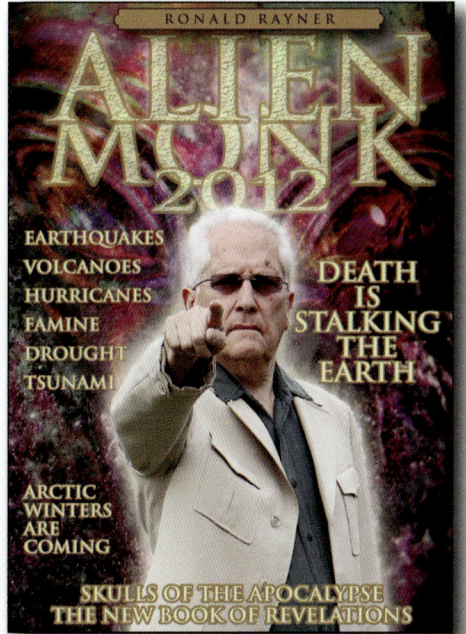

Amazon Kindle

CRAIG ALLEN RAYNER
Tibetan Travelling Shaman Monk

UK DISTRIBUTOR
Add Design
Telephone: (UK) 0845-6436395
E-Mail: info@add-design.co.uk

GARDNERS BOOKS
1 Whittle Drive, Eastbourne
East Sussex. BN23 6QH United Kingdom
Customer Care Telephone: (UK) 01323-521777

ISBN: 978-0-9573939-0-5

PUBLISHER
Blackthorn Publishing Ltd.,
Suite 404, Albany House, 324-326 Regent Street, London, W1B 3HH, United Kingdom.
Telephone: (UK) 01621-743882

SPIRITUAL & METAPHYSICAL POETRY
JETSUN KUSHO **Chapter 49**
SOME OTHER WORLD **Chapter 51**
MAGIC FOOTSTEPS **Chapter 52**
THE SQUARE OF PEGASUS **Chapter 57**
FROZEN WATERS **Chapter 58**
By
Sylvia Gladys Rayner
Lady of Annesley Grange

Design & Creation of Front & Back Covers
All Creative Photography, Makeup & Editing
By
Craig Allen Rayner

PRINTERS
Colt Press Ltd., Unit 7C Perry Road, Witham, Essex, CM8 3UD, United Kingdom.

To Ray, Best Wishes from Craig Rayner

FOREWORD

This book is mind blowing because it reveals that using his rare Crystal Skulls for Visual Scrying, the world's greatest Mystic and Prophet has seen the visions in Future Time of mankind sitting on the edge of a precipice, circled by more uncertainties, unknowns and hidden variables than at any time since the rise of mankind.

What is revealed in the chapters of this book is an altogether different picture of Future Time to that which is currently understood by governments and scientists across the world.

Ronald Rayner has seen catastrophic changes in climates, severe Earthquakes that will snap a Tectonic Plate in two. Tsunamis, Volcanic Eruptions, Floods, Famine and Fires, that will displace millions of people; and cause societies to fall apart, triggering mass migration that will spill across borders, with consequences so far reaching that the scenes are unimaginable. The planet is drying out; crops will fail by drought or be destroyed by fire, and massive dust storms carrying the very substance for the agriculture for some countries, will blow across the planet.

Present day global communications will ensure that news of intercontinental problems will spread to every part of the globe causing panic in world financial centres that will uncover big flaws in government finances; revealing that Treasuries have been emptying continuously due to severe economic crisis surrounding them, to which there appears to be no end in sight, all triggering a temporary financial panic and worldwide financial collapse.

The Psyche of man will change as he sees Armageddon for him personally unfolding before his very eyes, and realises that global businesses and banks, aided by sophisticated advertising have been lying and stealing from him for decades in order to produce a fine living for themselves; a realisation that will raise social unrest across the world.

Sylvia Gladys Rayner

INDEX

PROLOGUE

SEE THE FUTURE REALITY OR DIE BECAUSE THE BOOK OF REVELATIONS WILL BE FULFILED

Seers and Prophets

Years of devotion to right living, right thinking, plus the choice of celibacy has enabled me to reach the high spiritual awareness that allows me to achieve a non-ordinary state of mind, free from egotistical yearnings for my transformation into Seer, Mystic, and Prophet, probably best explained as someone who is able to capture events in advance of the events happening, also knowledge of the contents in Future Time before it arrives. A non-ordinary state of Mind must not be thought upon as being a distorted state of Reality, but the ability to see other Realities that are equally as valid as present Reality.

Seers are born, not made, and there are no short cuts to Mysticism and Prophesy. A Mystic is someone who can step outside present Mind, and look into a Reality of Mind in Future Time. The natural progress from Mysticism leads to Prophesy, the instrument for seeing and thus predicting change, using a developed pattern of Mind above the settled pattern of thought, circumventing or seeing over the normal pattern of Mind in order to interpret future natural phenomena. We who can achieve this are few and we are certainly rare. It should be noted that when possible my Forecasts and Predictions are checked against the latest relevant scientific data on the chosen subject, a system that my books reveal and confirm as having achieved a record of one hundred per cent accuracy in my forecasting and predictive work.

When I feel the need to look into Future Time either as the result of a dream or a strong psychic prompting, I do so using my trusted method of Visual Scrying through one of my Crystal Skulls, such as my preferred 'God' skull, weighing in at over forty kilos is probably the largest crystal skull in the world. The future events that I have witnessed recently during Visual Scrying are both profound and give cause for concern.

1

Future Survival Of Mankind
Is Uncertain

Perhaps the most significant of the markers for future events coming round for the planet during December 2012, is that the movement of the planets around the sun will render the future for mankind on Planet Earth more uncertain than at any time in the past one hundred and twenty five thousand years. It is clear that the minor variations in the Earth's rotations around the sun that occurred regularly in the past has completed its cycle, and the new cycle will drive changes in Earth's weather patterns not seen for thousands of years. Added into these circumstances, are the combined effects of manmade Global Warming across the planet, which in December 2012 passes its tipping point, indicating that there will be no sea ice in the Arctic by 2015.

As a Seer I have seen confirmation that dark natural changes and forces within the Solar System are gathering to fetch the fulfilment of THE BOOK OF REVELATIONS; forces that will alter established world weather patterns dramatically endangering the lives of literally millions of people on planet Earth, countless millions of whom will be lost.

Zigzag Earthquakes
and
Virtual Reality

As I have already made clear, there will be dramatic and traumatic events coming along in Future Time, on a scale never before seen. Whilst these events are in progress, the World will be struck by Armageddon. Parts of the planet will almost be rent in two. Islands will disappear, and the land will be raised up. There will be dry land where an Ocean once stood, and an Ocean will open up where there was once dry land. All the Tectonic Plates will move, triggered rare reverberating zigzag earthquakes along the Plates, some deep in the oceans setting off marine earthquakes along old fault lines.

The purpose of this book is to explain what is coming from the near future for the benefit of those amongst you who feel that 'forewarned is forearmed', because most people across the developed world are largely ignorant of that which is coming from the near future, and would in any event prefer to remain in denial. This can be explained as largely due to the influences of Television and Television Advertising using its powers and knowledge to alter people's perception of 'truth'. Television achieves this by overwriting that which people know to be true with new manipulated data and information that looks true, to the point where 'Virtual' is substituted for 'Real'. Bombarded by this 'Virtual'; falsehood lulls readers and viewers into unwittingly losing their true life judgements so that they are eventually captured in a Surrealist World, most of the time, where an ordinary breakfast cereal is presented almost as an essential daily medicine.

The EU Concept Is Flawed In Its Present Form and Armageddon Will Surround Pensions and The Unemployed

I can say with confidence that the closure of 2012 marks the beginning of dramatic changes for most European Economies. European Economies started their rise in the year 1066, reaching their peak in the year 2000, after which the line on my graph passed over the peak and started into a scale of one thousand years of continuous slow economic contraction and decline across Europe with short lived upturns. This scenario has serious implications for the long term value of share holdings, property values and pension values. The expectation of continuous increases in the value of shares held in pension schemes, for private individuals, plus the value of retail property pension schemes, is a thing of the past, and will no longer apply in Future Time. As for general Pension arrangements, after subtracting annual charges and fees, many of which will not be revealed to the pension holders, the final value of pensions in the UK in Future Time will be abysmally low, coincident with food prices reaching all time record highs. Looking at a recent example of pension performance in Holland for example, and comparing the result with the United Kingdom: A male aged thirty living in Holland, paying the same Pension Contribution Annually as a UK contributor; both retiring at 65 years, the draw down for the pensioner in Holland was fifty per cent higher than the draw down for the pensioner living in the UK. There is clearly an ethical problem in the UK which needs to be addressed by government.

A large increase in the incidence of natural disasters worldwide will hit disaster Insurers very hard, such as the cost of the US Drought, and some Companies may not survive, which will trigger a roll-on effect on pension values in the US.

Worldwide Scarcity Of Food

World farming and economies rely upon the regular weather patterns they have always enjoyed, particularly during their growing seasons. This is not going to happen in future! Extremely variable weather, drought conditions or excessive rainfall will become a permanent feature in many parts of the world. As a result World harvests will fall by at least fifty per cent. I warned about this in my last two books but it will not become in your face evident until 2013, and the consequences will be far reaching, even devastating in some parts of the world, leading to mass migration; societies will be torn apart by riots over food prices, and the problem will spill across borders.

Papering Over The Cracks Does Not Change The Facts

In my previous book, I predicted that unless and until the European Bank becomes a lender of last resort to EU countries such as Spain and Italy, the Euro could collapse, forcing the Bank into the position where it has to take up the mantle of Lender of Last Resort. Take care when this event takes place not to be misled. Nothing of the fundamentals is changed. The basic idea for the construction of the EU is flawed. No one will ever convince me that the Greek Economy warrants the same currency value as Germany, or that Spain warrants the same currency value as Germany. As long as the Members of the European Union remain living in a Walter Mitty World believing otherwise, the EU is destined for long term disintegration.

Property Values Will Fall Into The Foreseeable Future

O ver future years most European Economies (and economies across the world) will continue to slowly and imperceptibly shrink across different sectors of their economies. The long lasting boom in high value goods has finished. Starting with small companies, shopping outlets (fifty per cent will close), which has serious implications for the values of some Pension Funds. The value of regional commercial properties will fall in value continuously over time. More and more retail properties will remain empty due to a fundamental change towards retail shops occupying a smaller footprint, reduced by as much as sixty percent in some areas. This contagion will move on to infect larger businesses as the general public continue towards less and less disposable income to spend on anything other than essentials such as food. Stagnation in European Economies, and negative growth in the obvious areas in Europe, and dysfunctional government agencies not fit for purpose, will drag European Economies down to experiencing unemployment levels not seen since the nineteen thirties. The economic slowdown will spread across the industrialised world, affecting countries like China and Japan.

What To Do About High Street and Shopping Centre Closures

U nless and until Councils and Retail Property Companies realise they will need to put money into keeping High Street and Shopping Centres alive, closure of Retail Premises will exceed fifty per cent. What to do!

(A) Governments and Councils must introduce without delay TWO YEAR APPRENTICESHIPS IN RETAIL SALES AND SERVING IN RESTAURANTS. In a bid to make many of the unemployed school leavers fit to serve older customers buying in shops and visiting restaurants.

(B) Attract the fast growing population of older people to High Streets and Shopping Centres by making their visit a pleasant experience, with people fit to serve them, and places to sit and relax to sort out shopping. Easy accessible parking where the first hour is Free, and the second hour costs only twenty pence. With a Two hour limit.

(C) The biggest uphill task is facing High Street Retailing, because shops that have closed in High Streets will never return. A whole new era in retailing experience, combined with internet shopping and a change in the profile of shoppers is on our doorstep. By 2018 the majority of shoppers will come from older people and people over fifty, and the elderly, because the young will not have any money left over after buying food, because most will remain unemployed, with the exception of the few school leavers supported by their parents.

(D) Attract shops with Niche Markets. Internet Shopping is only fifteen per cent of all retail sales. However, buying on the Internet, and collecting from High Street Shopping Centres will grow rapidly, Why not make the visit a pleasant experience to attract the 'collectors' to return.

Values Of Higher End Residential Properties Will Continue To Fall Slowly Over A Long Time Span

People throughout the EU will have less disposable income, and this will impinge on the higher end of property markets. People living in five and six bedroom houses will find them almost impossible to sell, because there will not be sufficient people around with the money available to buy. The 'nest egg' people were relying upon for their retirement from the sale of their higher end property, is not going to happen. Higher priced properties will fall back to the price level at which they were purchased twenty years ago. The longer people hang on for a recovery that is never going to arrive, the lower the value to which their property will fall, and the lower the price they will have to accept when they need to sell. Property prices are never going to recover to the 2007 levels reached in the United Kingdom.

Rip Off Food Prices, Petrol and Diesel Prices, Plus Continuous Increases In Energy Costs Will Drive Pensioners and The Unemployed Into Poverty

Many pensioners and the unemployed will move into poverty as the hidden costs of living rises to between twenty and thirty per cent per annum, fetched stealthily by smaller tins, smaller packages, lower weights and volumes in the previous size packaging, but all sold at the same price as previously. Here is my own personal example. Less than a year ago I bought a packet of porridge breakfast cereal at a cost of two pounds. In 2012 the cost has risen to three pounds for the same size packet and weight, or a rise of thirty per cent! I could put forward a whole basket of goods purchased in a Supermarket costing between twenty to thirty per cent more than a year ago. In 2013 the cost of many food commodities will rise by greater than thirty per cent causing some foodstuffs to become luxury goods by price alone. What is the point, therefore, of powerful unions bringing workers out on strike for a two per cent pay rise, which in context renders strikes tantamount to a joke. It would be preferable for Unions to Lobby for greater transparency in Supermarket food pricing; the pricing of Petrol and Diesel; energy costs, and Regulators with guts and teeth. Lobby for Directors and other Elected people both in Business. Government and Local Government, who use their position to gain pecuniary advantage, deceive and cheat working people to gain fine living for themselves; to go to Prison and face unlimited personal fines and confiscation of personal assets.

Britain Should Organise A Northern European Union Before Ending Up In The Same Debt Scenario As Spain

A Northern European Union, for example, comprising Ireland, UK, Sweden, Denmark, Norway and parts of the former Soviet Union, plus an Accord and Alliance with North and South America would fetch a rosy future for all members of such a union. The old European Union, which is fundamentally flawed, pretending that The Greek, Spanish and Cypriot economies all have the same economic and currency values as Germany; there is no hope. As long as the European Union continues to 'pass the Joker' pretending it has a value, powerful and successful nations across the world looking in at the European Union, and seeing it paralysed by every small problem it appears unable to resolve, will continue to lose respect for the European Union and the Euro. An alternative financially solid New Northern European Union with a North and South American Alliance, taking advantage of Russia's Membership of the World Trade Organisation, would rise and rise.

When the present Coalition Government took office in the United Kingdom, it inherited the most massive debt built up by a previous government in peace time Britain. By 2012 effective measures and new legislation have been put into place to control and reduce Government debt. However, as a punishment for these responsible actions and measures, the Coalition is likely to lose office after the General Election in 2015. If the present attitude of the Government Opposition is any guide; talk of strikes and plans for a General Strike, when the opposition takes over Government, there will be another 'free for all' in Public Sector Pay and Pensions that will build up debt on a massive scale, and by 2020 Britain will find itself in the same position that Greece and Spain occupy today. That is the longer term future for the United Kingdom. There is no hope.

Continuous Unrelenting Rise In Unemployment Inevitable

It should be obvious from the predictions in my books that the scene is set for a continuous slow unrelenting rise in unemployment across the European Union as a whole, and other parts of the Western World, interrupted only by seasonal fluctuations. The UK Government is putting measures in place to alleviate the plight of young unemployed. Do not be misled by the heralding of the take up of jobs in Europe, because the majority of new jobs will be part time employment on minimum wage. European Union Employment Directive and Minimum Wage Directives only exacerbate the problems, with the 'one brush fits all' approach to businesses and economies large or small; plus the silent continuous effect of Automation and Computerisation across all areas of business; companies reassessing working practices in the light of the Internet and Digital Revolution, continuously reducing the numbers of people needed to complete many tasks; changing the status of many jobs to part time, is guaranteed to burden future unemployment figures.

Seventy Five Percent Of Young Unemployed In The World Will Never Work

According to my own calculations, seventy five percent of young people leaving education within the United Kingdom and the rest of the European Union will not find work in the areas for which they have studied and completed degree courses for far into the future. The cumulative year on year numbers will be staggering. Albeit that the UK Government is tackling this problem, but in my opinion is swimming against the tide.

The Time For Farmers Has Come

The only exception will be in food production. The time for Farmers has come, and it is time for the importance of their contribution to food security in the UK to be recognised, because the farming industry will need to expand production to meet future demand for food to offset the rise in the prices of costly imports. Southern Ireland should be courted by the United Kingdom for the difference its excellent quality foods could make to United Kingdom Food supplies. Ukraine, a country friendly to Britain, has vast areas of underused high quality agricultural land; a subject that needs to be looked into seriously by the UK farming industry, because it could be a life saver as world food production and supplies start to fail dramatically due to unexpected variations in weather patterns; extreme rainfall or drought across the world, plus unexpected arctic type Winter weather events occurring in North America and Northern Europe.

War Over Water

The only nation in the world that is making plans to feed its peoples and provide sufficient drinking water for the future is China. That nation is far more advanced than the rest of the world, surrounding the Indian Ocean, for example, with Towns and Ports, agricultural areas and Fish Farms drawing into China much of the product that was previously exported to Europe and America. China is also constructing a massive Naval Base to protect their interests in the region. [I have forecast that fish will disappear from most areas of the Indian Ocean by 2014.] China is following a similar policy in Africa, where nations like Uganda and Nigeria are booming, while the peoples of other areas such as the Horn of Africa continue to suffer the effect of overpopulation, water stress and famine on a massive scale, placing as many as twenty million people at risk. Nevertheless, China will start to legitimately take for itself, products that were previously exported to Europe and America.

China will secure its drinking water supplies for far into the future by diverting rivers and building dams to control the flow from the Himalaya, the source of drinking water for over ten per cent of the world's population. Plans for these numerous developments are at an advanced stage. Some of the nations in the world that will be affected by reduced water supply from the Himalaya are living in denial. In Future Time, one or two of these nations will use their Air Forces to destroy some of China's newly built Dams; actions that will lead to a war only China can win.

Ten Per Cent Or More Of World Population Will Suffer Water Stress In 2013

Major pollution of the water supply from the Himalaya running through India; their sacred Ganges will also suffer reduced flow exacerbating the extent of serious pollution. Overpopulation will drive a Great Plague across India. The people will suffer sores and puss on their faces and bodies; millions will die. Weak infrastructure for Power Supplies and drinking water will fail from time to time, damaging the Indian economy. Bangladesh continues to suffer serious overpopulation causing it to run into drinking water stress; there are areas of serious pollution, sea level rise and food shortages.

Corruption across every aspect of life in India that keeps half the population below the poverty line has reached a point where it will drown out India's explosive economic growth, and lead to civil unrest as major world Supermarket Groups push millions of small traders into poverty. The economic sun may have put his hat on over India.

Available drinking water will also dry up in areas of the Middle East, which will lead to rumours of war.

Severe Winter Weather Events Coming To North America, Scandinavia, Scotland and The United Kingdom

Melt water from the melting ice in the Arctic flowing into the North Atlantic is slowing the Atlantic Conveyor by up to thirty per cent, eventually lowering Winter temperatures over Scotland and parts of the UK, triggering Winter weather events that will have a temporary adverse roll on effect on some economies. Tail end Hurricanes arriving from the South Atlantic will come across Ireland, Western England and Scotland.

The warming of the Atlantic Ocean is giving off heat as the melt water and warm water collide, and this heat is rising to increase cloud cover and wind; rising further to a height of sixty kilometres. On the Eastern side of the Globe, the Warming of the Indian Ocean is also giving off heat. Increasing cloud cover and wind moving North from this region will also rise to interfere with the jet stream above the arctic, punching holes in the circular Westerly winds which will allow Siberian winds through, forcing Arctic Weather down to thirty degrees. Thus causing Severe Winter Weather events to arrive into Northern Europe, North America, Scotland and the United Kingdom; **the big snow!** If weather forecasters send instruments high above the North Pole, accurate forecasting of the arrival of these severe winter events should be possible.

World Food Supplies
Edging Towards Apocalypse

I have reserved my end chapter of this Prologue for my most serious warning yet: **SEE THE FUTURE OR DIE**. In my previous book I warned about and predicted serious increased rainfall in the UK, but more importantly, I warned about a major shift in the world weather patterns that would fetch prolonged drought that would last over seven hundred years in the USA, and parts of South America. The continuous drought will have a major effect across twelve states, including Missouri, Texas, Oklahoma, Kansas etc. The result is that both crops and meat product will fall by fifty percent each year, and the reduction will continue and become cumulative over the following years. The cumulative effect in the Mid West will return the soil to a dust bowl: similar conditions also to be suffered in Australia, Ukraine, and the Russia's, reducing food supplies across the world significantly. Unrest will rise across the Globe as food shortages and unaffordable prices become apparent. Millions will be on the move across borders in search of food and clean drinking water, and further millions will starve to death before reaching food and water; all an integral part of the pattern of Apocalypse lying out there in Future Time.

OIL ARMAGEDDON

Iran is an Islamic country that has a research facility busily enriching uranium that Iran claims is for peaceful purposes, Iran has a perfect right so to do, but for the rest of the world the question remains, why is Iran enriching uranium/plutonium to a quality where the material can be used for assembling an atomic weapon? Experts have explained to me that Weapons grade material is not necessary for fuelling nuclear reactors that drive turbines to produce electricity.

The required level of enriched material that is necessary for constructing an Atomic Bomb will be reached by Iran in June 2013 or slightly before, after which point it will be possible for Iran's scientists to assemble an atomic weapon.

With this information to hand, the month of June in the year 2013, or before, will be "Make your Mind up Time" for the Israelis, for the following question; at what point does Israel, as a last resort, launch its well planned ground and air attack on the research facility/facilities in Iran, where the Atomic Bomb is being assembled.

Information from Iran claims that Iran's Special Forces have established many Bunker positions looking out over the Straits of Hormuz, with facilities from which to launch hundreds of missiles at the oil tankers passing through the Straits.

The Worlds Policemen, the USA, will be primed by Israel, before Israel launches an attack on Iran, to move the US 6th Fleet into the Straits of Hormuz, if it's not already positioned there, at which point oil suppliers will stop sending oil tankers through this short cut to major markets. Within a few days of this happening there would arise a crisis in the World Oil Market.

Russia is a country where the use of intelligence and stealth by its World Leader, President Putin, has enabled Russia to become a powerful member of the World Gas and Oil supply industries. Russia will benefit enormously from a hike in world energy prices, and is likely to sit contentedly on the sidelines as such a drama plays out. The USA has wisely manoeuvred itself into a good position for availability of energy internally but, for the rest of the world's major economies, Oil Armageddon, even for a short time, will push them deeper into recession.

It is my opinion that it is perfectly possible to enjoy democratic Islam anywhere in the world that will work for the benefit of everyone. Dare I suggest that Islamic extremism have almost reached its 'sell by date', and Oil Armageddon could be the Turning Point.

NOW READ THIS. The purpose of this book in the Alien Monk Series it to warn readers that THE BOOK OF REVELATIONS written by St John on the Isle of Patmos nearly two thousand years ago will be fulfiled. A new Book of Revelations is written.

Ronald Rayner London, June, 2012.

CHAPTER 49

A SHADOW IS BEING CAST OF DEVASTATION TO COME IN FUTURE TIME FULFILMENT OF REVELATIONS

During my studies and fascination with the subject of Mysticism, I have read and followed the work of famous Parapsychologist, Carl Jung, and carried out my own research into his ideas. Uncovering by accident the nature and method of Scrying used by Seer Nostradamus and how he was able to use his own method of Scrying to make his predictions of major events that would occur in Future Time. The enormous advantage I enjoy over these great characters from history is being able to check my predictions against the latest scientific findings.

One of the interesting findings by Carl Jung was that most, if not all, important events in world history, 'Cast a Shadow before the Event', and my own research as an independent scientist confirms his findings. I am aware that at the present time, many people are experiencing feelings welling up inside them from their subconscious mind that they are unable to explain such as the feeling – dark clouds are gathering - the bad is coming. Many People are also at a loss to explain the bad behaviour by people around them, even friends and neighbours, including their own children.

In my books in the Alien Monk series, I write about the unthinkable, the unexpected, events that people think will never happen, and yet everything I write is based on a scientific truth. This combination has enabled me to score one hundred percent accuracy for my forecasts and predications in my past books. These successes have taught me to soak up flattery and praise from around the world like a sponge, whilst ignoring my critic.

MYSTICISM HELPS TO SEE THROUGH THE CLOUDS INTO FUTURE TIME

It is not easy to make unpleasant truths read like a novel, but my interest and study of mysticism helps, because mysticism is a pre condition for serious and critical thought to interrogate life and science more deeply in my search for ultimate truths.

One thing my research has revealed to me is that the average human mind automatically takes everything as having always existed, and will never change, which means that people in general know nothing about events out there in Future Time that could have a dramatic downside influence on everything they love and value.

The concept of something upcoming and new on the horizon is difficult for people to grasp, more particularly if that which is upcoming and new is unpleasant, in which case they take the easy route of ignoring the things they do not like. People choosing to take this route are ignoring that old adage, 'forewarned is forearmed', and yet evolution exists on the premise that organisms, for example, develop something new, whilst maintaining a continuation.

Even politicians around the world cherry pick from important scientific reports the bits that actually promote their own causes, leaving the general public totally ignorant of other important scientific information and detail contained in those reports, to which public attention should be drawn, because there is a danger that their very existence could be threatened.

The information contained in my Books in the 'Alien Monk' series should be important to everyone's personal welfare and survival in Future Time. If I describe to readers the nature of Time, it will help readers understand the information contained in the all important third chapter of this book, knowledge that is unlikely to be found elsewhere. Dark natural forces are coming together in our Solar System the result of which will contribute to dramatically changing many economies across the planet, fetching deprivation, hardship, shortages of food, and starvation to millions.

*Aristocratic Tibetan Woman from Shigatse
wearing regional costume and
carrying a hunting purse with bullets.*

JETSUN KUSHO

Once Upon a Time
In the Himalaya
The Heart of a Tibetan Girl
Slowed to a Soft Beat
And Finally Stopped.

Deep in Meditation
Deep in Snow.

As she Entered the Dream World
The Orbs of Heaven greeted her,
Sweet Music from the Spheres,
The girl Began her Journey.

She saw the Brightness of the Lights.
Her eyes Wide in Wonder.

Surely this is not Death,
Listen To Me.

TELL MY BROTHERS,
I AM NOT DEAD.

SWEET SISTER you have entered
THUMO RESKIANG.
You have Left your Body
There on the slopes of CHOMOLUNGMO.

Your Body is Protected
By the Great Spirit Healer.
Your Heart is Rested
Waiting for your Return.

First you must travel
To the World of Good
The World of Evil.

18

THERE are Angels to Protect you.
SPIRITS TO WATCH OVER YOU.
ANCESTORS to guide you.

ENJOY the wonders of the Cosmos
As you Seek the Truth.

TAKE these memories with you
Soon you will Enter your Earthly Body
To return Once Again to your
Beloved Mountains.

Pray with us Dear Sister
As you Greet the New Day,
Remember Us in the Spirit World.

WE ARE ALWAYS WITH YOU.

NOW SHE UNDERSTOOD

THE SPHERES Greeted Her
With their Sweet Music
Enchanting her with Magic and Mystery.

SHE WAS NOW ONE
WITH THE MOUNTAIN

Dedicated to Alexandra David-Neel (1868-1969)
Who is now One with the Mountain.

Sylvia Gladys Rayner 2012

WORLD ECONOMIES ARE SET ON A COURSE FOR SLOW COLLAPSE

This book describes the long term changes that are coming around in our Solar System arriving after December 2012, and the devastation that these changes will fetch across the globe from the BRINGING ABOUT OF THE FULFILMENT OF THE BOOK OF REVELATIONS written around two thousand years ago by a Disciple of the Prophet Jesus. Changes in our Solar System are on the way. The actual effects will take the form of devastating Earthquake that will rent a Tectonic Plate in two, Storms, Massive Tsunami, Volcanic Eruptions, Flooding, Forest Fires, Famine, Shortages of Clean Drinking Water in many countries; increase in the number and severity of Hurricanes. Siberian Winters arriving across Scotland, the North of England, and other parts of Europe and North America, Storm Force Winds and Rain arriving across South West England and the North from the North Atlantic. Also creeping almost undetected until recent times but clearly predicted in my previous books, are factors that will bring about the slow deterioration of European and other important World Economies, all coming together on a scale not previously seen in the history of developed nations on the Earth at this time.

MYSTICISM CAN EXPLAIN HOW TO BUILD A GOOD OR BAD FUTURE FROM THE PAST AND THE PRESENT

Consider that; The leading edge of Time is the personal Model of Reality given in our Mind (Brain). The Past has been, and while it no longer exists in Now it still exists in the Model of Reality in our Mind. The Future has yet to come and so does not exist in Now. The Past is memory that lingers on in the Model of Reality in our Mind. The Future is anticipation, but will exist in the Model of future Reality in our Mind. The Now, the Present, is a direct conscious experience of encounter with the world around us as constructed for us personally as the Model of Reality in our Mind. We in the Present can think of the Future because of the Model of Future Reality can be constructed by our Brain. Now, however, is the Model of the continuous reality of the Present, whereas the Past is a memory of a previous Reality in our Mind that has been eaten up by Time.

The Future is on the other side of the leading edge of Time. Now, contains the seeds being planted from which future synchronicity will grow. Future synchronicity thus grows from actions in the present, thus the future also exists in a form in the here and now. All the Futures are coming at us, but it is our thoughts, and actions, and Synchronicity created by our behaviour within our Model of Reality of 'Now', that enables 'All the Futures' to resolve into 'One Future', influenced by our thoughts and actions Now and in the past. [Entropy dictates that everything moves from order to chaos revealing that the Arrow of Time always moves in one direction, from past to future].

Every human being builds their future Synchronicity, good or bad for them personally, by their actions in the past, and in the present. 'Now', that is to say, the way in which they lead their daily life will shape their Synchronicity; the events that will unfold for them in their Model of Reality created by their Brain in Future Time. Synchronicity is the coming together of these events or happenings at an instant of time in the future for Good or for Bad, but we created the happening ourselves from events of the past. So it is with whole Nations and Governments across the Planet.

THE POWERS OF THE UNIVERSE WILL WIPE AWAY HUMANS AND WHOLE NATIONS THAT ARE DESTROYING THE PLANET AND NOT ADVANCING THE FUTURE IMPROVEMENT IN THE DEVELOPMENT OF HUMAN KIND

Human Beings and Governments enjoy the gift of Free Will, albeit within the constraints of the social class and circumstance into which they are born or come together, and for individuals, the genes they have inherited. This enables people and governments to enjoy the choice of breaking away from the norm to achieve good synchronicity, but if they exercise Free Will in the wrong way, they will build up bad synchronicity for themselves out there in Future Time, and in the case of governments, nations that build bad Synchronicity will take them down to destruction.

The end result is that individuals and whole nations will NOT enjoy a continuous future in Time and Eternity. These are the Laws of the Prophets. Our planet, the living cell, will wipe away all that is bad and poisoning the planet. The same considerations apply for human kind, Human kind that retreats back towards the animal state from its evolved developed condition, have no purpose or use on the planet in Future Time, and will be wiped away. Those individuals and governments that have built good Synchronicity (Karma) will survive the devastation that lies ahead because events and happenings will come together that will fall to their favour. No Nation will remain untouched by the events coming in Future Time. The Maya reveal how the will of the Powers of the Universe is brought about.

The rotation of the planets within our Universe, and the Solar System itself, are locked within a relatively fixed Past, Present and Future. All acting like cogs locked together turning in a huge machine. According to the Maya, everything is coming together to end a complete three hundred and sixty degree cycle and starting again from square one.

MAJOR CHANGE COMING IN THE SOLAR CYCLE

During a cycle, an invisible gear can move a cog slightly out from the adjoining cogs, whilst remaining within the cogs of the whole system, enabling a Moon, Planet or Sun to move slightly away from its neighbours in regular repeatable long term cycles. The sun, for example, can become less active due to a lesser hidden rotation within the main rotation, all eventually returning to a tightly fitting cog over a fixed cycle. It is these movements, however tiny, that will cause major changes to take place on planet Earth that can wipe away the whole or part of Human and Animal life. These events happen in regular long term continuous cycles contained within a long term time scale beyond normal comprehension, explained in the second chapter of this book.

Earthquakes, Volcanic Eruptions, Tsunamis, Flooding, Hurricanes, plus Severe Weather and Weather Events on a scale not seen in the past will bring about serious disruption to Economies across the Globe. No one has yet calculated the Trillions of dollars that will be lost.

Scientists using Super Computers will be fully aware of the changes coming about in our Solar System that Governments are powerless to stop or delay. It is of course easier for governments to turn a 'blind eye' than to spend the monies necessary, at a time when many governments across the world are short of money, to make the necessary preparations towards the alleviation of the problems ahead.

The United States of America has developed the most powerful super computers in the world. That nation will be fully aware of changes that are coming around in our Solar System that man is powerless to stop or prevent. This is most likely to be the reason why America has stepped back on the issue of Global Warming. The American government and our American cousins are fully capable of standing tall and overcoming any catastrophe that may hit that Nation.

Shaman Artifacts to Influence Good Fortune

CHAPTER 50

PERSONAL ANXIETY TRIGGERED BY DEVASTATION AND DESTRUCTION WITNESSED DURING SESSIONS OF VISUAL SCRYING AS I SAW THE BEGINNING OF THE FULFILMENT OF THE BOOK OF REVELATIONS

I Awoke with the first shimmer of daylight peeping through my bedroom curtains, which was the trigger for thoughts and messages to start spilling into my mind. Sometimes I find it difficult to contain all the information coming through, and then I worry that I will not have sufficient time to write down everything before the details are forgotten. That leads on to the anxious thought that I may have missed some important psychic message that will be lost forever.

I was feeling very emotional about the things that I was seeing during my sessions of Visual Scrying over the last few days; the destruction of huge numbers of human and animal life on a scale never before seen, and desolation spreading across many continents. All of which made me feel vulnerable. My mind was in a whirl wondering what to do. My thoughts and feelings felt unusually profound. It was becoming impossible for me to remain detached, just observing every scene of devastation and destruction playing out before me in Future Time in vivid technicolour.

This was the first time since I began the art of Visual Scrying that I felt it was impossible for me to write down and record the sheer volume of everything I was witnessing. The volume was just too great. All so many sights so many staggering events. How would it be possible for such a mass of information to be contained within the mind of a single person. There would surely never be sufficient time to record everything I had seen.

PREPARING FOR THE FIRST NEW BOOK OF REVELATIONS TO SUPERSEDE THE REVELATIONS WRITTEN BY ST JOHN 2000 YEARS IN THE PAST

I was feeling desperate, and with no one to whom I could turn, I knew I had to visit Sun Lin, my Alien Monk in the Himalaya, and ask for his help and advice. It would be pointless talking to anyone on planet Earth, because it is my experience that most people in general know very little about Visual Scrying, Mysticism or Prophesy.

None had experienced the evolutionary jump I have suffered. Sun Lin is the only person I can trust. That one person I can rely upon. I would ask him if I was really seeing the days of judgement; the wicked generation being wiped away, perhaps the beginning of the end. I would also ask Sun Lin if he would relieve me of the task of writing the first new Book of Revelation, since the Revelations written by St John on the Isle of Patmos two thousand years ago. After all, Sun Lin would know that in spite of the record of one hundred per cent accuracy in my Predictions, no one on Earth would believe a word I would write. What would be the point!

The peoples of the so called advanced nations across Europe have grown new National Identities; drowning in 'binge drinking', drunkenness, obesity, drug taking, adultery and bad parenting, nevertheless, like Sodom and Gomorrah, who would believe that the days of judgement are on their way to planet Earth, except for the handful of us who have seen the visions of the apocalypse ahead with our own eyes.

I would also need to admit to Sun Lin that I had strayed from his teachings that must be obeyed when entering sessions of Visual Scrying, 'Observe what you see only Ronald, keeping the mind blank. Do not under any circumstances pay attention to thoughts, feelings, judgements and emotions that stray into your mind about what you are observing. For your own sanity you must remain the observer only Ronald, but you must write down everything you see in as much detail as possible for Future History'.

My lapse in ignoring the rules given to me by Sun Lin has caused me to suffer the emotional consequences. I felt the need to flee to Sun Lin as soon as possible.

I also felt really stupid inside because this is the first occasion on which my vulnerability when Visual Scrying had surfaced.

Looking from my bedroom window, the sun was shining, not a cloud in the sky and the trees were in the full bloom of early spring. Yes. This was a day that God had made for me to take a crystal God Skull into my garden with Wilson my skeleton and prepare for trance meditation into Visual Scrying to go on my journey to the Himalaya to visit my Alien Monk Sun Lin in his workshop, and ask him to reveal the answers to puzzles that have been racing around in my mind.

It dawned on me it was time to get moving. Down to breakfast, a bowl of porridge to keep my cholesterol low made with goats milk, mix in a spoonful of cod liver oil for my bones, a spoonful of honey for its antibacterial properties, a sprinkling of powdered zinc to boost my immune system, vitamin B12 for my nervous system, all topped off with cinnamon powder to keep colds at bay. Truly the elixir of life followed by a four minute egg and toasted soldiers prepared by my wife Sylvia. Rinse off the cutlery and plates, pop them in the dishwasher and make a cup of coffee. After digesting everything my day could begin. However, I felt quite gluttonous when I remembered that my youngest son, Craig Allen Rayner, a Survivalist, could live off a soup of wild herbs, with earth worms and grubs mixed in to provide protein. On occasions little more than a few mouthfuls of wild herbs when he is travelling in the Himalaya taking photographs for the Alien Monk series of books, and climbing into caves in the Himalaya looking for bones and any other evidence of visits by aliens. Craig can survive for days on a few mouthfuls of wild herbs, and herb tea. I consoled myself with the thought that my weight is normal for my height.

PREPARING FOR VISUAL SCRYING USING A CRYSTAL SKULL

Once again it was time to get started on setting out the artefacts necessary for my Visual Scrying and Trance Meditation when I would journey to see Sun Lin in Tibet. I marked out a circle on my lawn fifteen feet in diameter, facing the rising sun. I collected my Singaporean table from the conservatory and two Victorian chairs with arms, placing them side by side behind the table. The next task was to collect a Crystal Skull, and offer it to the North, South, East and West, in turn, and place it on the table within my reach. Then came the difficult and rather delicate task of moving Wilson my skeleton from his seat at our dining table. Carrying him into the garden and placing him on the chair next to me, dressed in his full Tibetan priestly outfit.

I went into the house to fetch my largest Crystal Skull, the 'God' Skull, so named because it weighed in at over forty kilos, and it is said to have been carried inside an Ark with carrying poles on either side, all of which had long since disintegrated. Whilst my 'God' skull was the Crystal Skull of my choice for this session of Visual Scrying, I realised there was no way I could lift over forty kilos, and carry it into my garden. My choice of the 'God' Skull rested on the story that it was once carried in the Ark of the Covenant, together with the Tablets brought down from the Mountain by the great Prophet Moses. During my first session of Visual Scrying with the 'God' Skull, I was awe struck by a vision of the Prophet Moses in vivid colour standing in his robes holding two large Tablets. Such was the impression that the vision made upon me that I committed the vision to oil on canvas, less I forget that wonderful scene.

In a change of plan I decided to use the Tibetan Skull, the largest clear Crystal Skull originally based in Tibet. A skull of significance because it is said to complete, 'The Circle of Seven Skulls', the coming together of which would signify that the end of the world is nigh which, and with hindsight, has proved to be significant.

THE RITUAL PREPARATION FOR VISUAL SCRYING

I carried the skull into the garden, offered it to the four corners of the Earth, before placing the skull onto the table within reach of my hands. I sat down next to Wilson, said The Lord's Prayer for protection clasping my piece of Calvary given to me by Sister Katarina who attended the Altar of Crucifixion in the Holy Sepulchre in Jerusalem, when I was making my Documentary 'Jerusalem' (DVD sold by Amazon). Craig stood as the Sentinel outside the circle to ensure that no one entered the circle when I was deep in trance meditation.

I quickly entered into a deep trance, and felt myself in space, and moving towards Italy. In Northern Italy I saw huge piles of rubble caused by an Originating Earthquake and aftershocks, with people rushing in all directions. The quake was exactly as I had predicted, at forty degrees north, the crossover point of Solar Radiation crossing Turkey which indicates that it is almost certain that there will be a Compensating Earthquake crossing through Greece into the North of Turkey, on to Iran where a reverberating earthquake will strike. In Future Time there is likely to be a very nasty Earthquake Storm across the Bosporus.

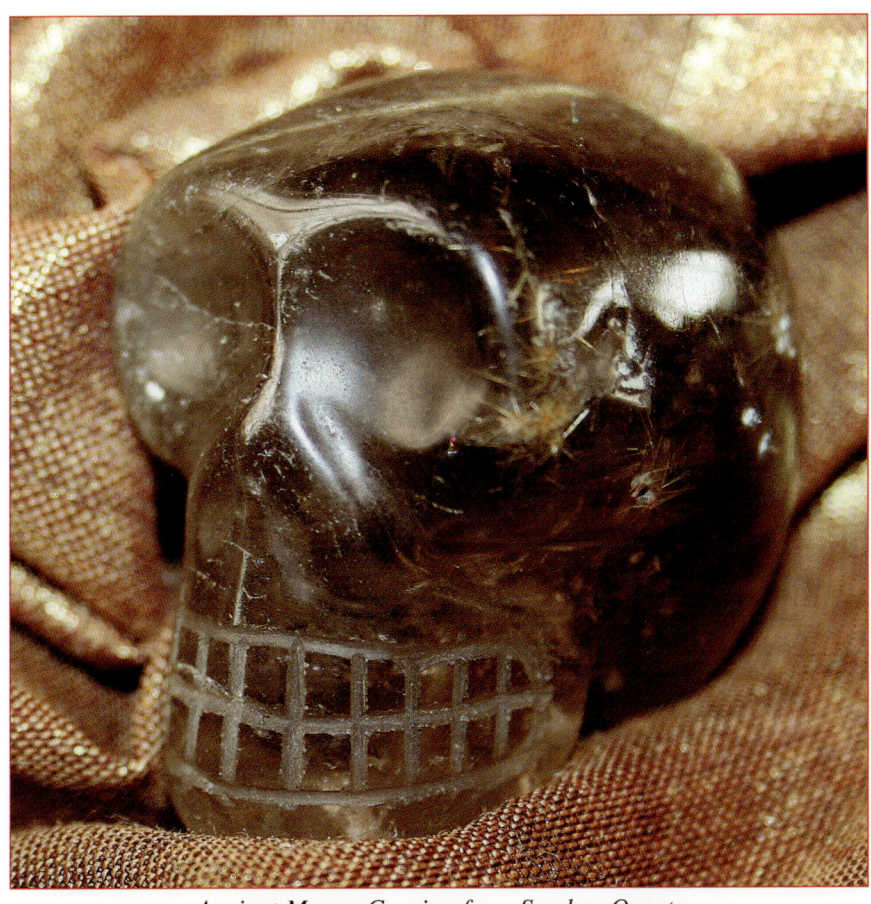

Ancient Mayan Carving from Smokey Quartz

CHAPTER 51

AN URGENT VISIT
TO ALIEN MONK SUN LIN
IN THE HIMALAYA

Once again I found myself flying across space towards the Himalaya to meet Sun Lin. Looking down I saw the flowers of the Himalaya, the Rhododendron in bloom. It was May, I passed a forest of Pine trees below peeping through the Himalayan snow. The valley was covered in Primula surrounding a forest of Rhododendrons. Higher up the slopes stood Magnolia trees topped with white Magnolia blossom glowing a blue white in the sunshine. As I rounded the snow pecks in the distance, I saw Sun Lin's Studio. To my astonishment Sun Lin appeared through a trap door onto the roof, and I landed gently on the roof standing beside him.

Wearing his usual smile on his ageless face, he spoke first. I was worried about you Ronald, and I am relieved that you hastened to come and visit me in your hour of need. You have learned the hard way, why not to break the rules I taught to you surrounding Visual Scrying, and the personal dangers associated with the phenomena.

There are few people in the world who can do what you do Ronald; a Seer who can visit Future Time, indeed they can be counted on one hand, but you Ronald will need to change or modify the way in which you think about the Function of Visual Scrying, and I will show the 'how'.

Come let us go down into the Studio to share some Yak Butter Tea, which I shall make for you in the traditional manner to celebrate your arrival, my special guest, because I have something important to relay to you.

MAKING YAK BUTTER TEA
USING THE TRADITIONAL METHOD

Sun Lin emptied tea leaves into a pot of boiled water, and poured the contents from the pot into a long narrow wooden cylinder, adding yak butter and salt, blending the ingredients together by working a plunger, after which the tea was then returned to the pot and reheated. This is the only true method of making Yak Butter Tea. I thought I would give you a treat Ronald with tasting a hot liquid as creamy as the Yak milk. After tasting the brew, I commented it was truly delicious Sun Lin, and the tea has warmed my whole body in seconds. You are truly a master of blending Yak Butter Tea.

What I want you to know Ronald is that your Predictions for the future of planet Earth in Future Time are truly amazing, because they are correct in every detail. So too is the course of events laid out in your Book of Revelations. What has amused me Ronald, is that in July 2011 on page twelve of your book 'Alien Monk 2012' (Amazon and Kindle) where you published the diabolical weather predictions for the United Kingdom; horrendous persistent rainfall, and flooding, also pinpointing the areas where the flooding would occur. All the while some Weather Experts were forecasting a hot dry summer, and the introduction of hose pipe bans!

INCORRECT WEATHER FORECASTING COST
INSURERS AND THE UK ECONOMY DEARLY

All the experts were wrong Ronald, and it is the all important farming communities who deserve so much better who suffer the consequences. Completely inadequate weather forecasting costs the United Kingdom economy dearly. World weather patterns have changed almost overnight; increased rainfall and extremes of weather are the future for the UK, to the point where the effects will impinge on Insurers and Agricultural Production. To add insult to injury, weather forecasters were claiming that it is impossible to predict the weather more than three weeks ahead. What utter rubbish Ronald, as you proved by publishing your forecast in print twelve months in advance of the events you predicted of extreme rainfall and flooding, following on from your success predicting the snowfall that would hit Scotland in the previous winter, completely missed by the forecasters, trapping hundreds of motorists in their vehicles, and yet it is all so simple to get it right. The scary part remains. The standard of forecasting does not bode well for the winter of 2012. I regret that nothing will change Ronald. Most institutions in the United Kingdom have been taught to follow the system, and I am told that 'Woe betides anyone who sticks their head above the wall'!

It is time now Ronald for me to reveal to you the secrets of what lies ahead in Future Time for Planet Earth. We will start first with the future for Space Travel, and then I will explain why new unexpected weather events are coming to planet Earth that will knock everyone sideways.

View of a Tibetan Kitchen

SOME OTHER WORLD

QUICK AS FIRE!
QUICK AS FIRE!

JINGLE BELLS RINGING.

The Letter Carrier
Speeding on his Mongolian Pony
Past our Camp and into the Night.

Blessings Brothers he Cried
Arms Waving
His voice disappearing.

As the Sun Rose in all its Glory
The Mountain shone Colours
Of the morning Mandala,
Rebirth had Begun.

We Ran to the Monastery
The garden full of Saffron Monks
Debating!
Swift with Questions!
Swift with Answers!

As I closed my eyes
And prayed to Buddha
I entered the Dream World
I had longed to see.

At first the Jingling of the Bells

Then the Power of the Earth

And the Quickness of the Fire

The Noble Eightfold Path
Clear to See
As I Journeyed into Time and Space.

The Stars, the Universe
No longer of this World.

Buddha Smiled as he gently
Carried me to the Waiting Monks.

They too Following the
Noble Eightfold Path.
Understanding a Boys Dream.

Sylvia Gladys Rayner 2012

URGENT NEED FOR A SELF SUFFICIENT SPACE STATION ON THE MOON PRODUCING OXYGEN, DRINKING WATER, ROCKET FUEL, GIANT TELESCOPES, FOOD PRODUCTION AND POWERFUL ROCKETS WITH NUCLEAR MANDLEBROT WARHEADS

When we last met Ronald, I promised to reveal to you the future for space exploration and the prospect of alien contact in Future Time. Unfortunately, we both became so excited and concerned about other issues to be discussed around the very survival of humanity on the planet over the next few years, other space matters were pushed aside to be discussed at a more convenient time.

At present Ronald, Earth's scientists are preoccupied with building a manned space craft in which astronauts will travel to planet Mars. At the present level of the technology and materials available on Earth, this is not a good plan. It is almost certain that such a manned craft could be hit by a mass solar ejection from the Sun during its nine month journey, and without the materials to protect both the technology and life on board; everything would be fried before the journeys end. That is without mentioning or considering the problems that will arise due to prolonged weightlessness, such as softening of bones and damage to eyesight.

Tell me Sun Lin, how will Human Kind escape from Earth in preparation for the future when the Moon has moved further away in its orbit from Earth, to a point where the stability of Earth that depends upon being held in place by the gravity of the Moon becomes less certain, leaving Earth constantly at risk of tilting to a new horizon, and unstable both Latitudinal and Longitudinally.

Everyone loves Astronomers Ronald, and it is for the Astronomers to step up to the plate Ronald and explain to scientists the importance of the Moon to the future of mankind. The priority should be not to send Astronauts on a perilous two hundred million miles plus journey to Mars at very high cost, but to build a self sustaining Space Station on the Moon. The next priority should be to assemble Telescopes, and use rockets launched from the Moon to land transmitting telescopes on Asteroids, from where they could gain a cost free ride round the Solar System, without risk to craft or Astronauts. Telescopes and a Super Computer set up on the Moon would collect all the information and data arriving from space and relay it to scientists on Earth.

No one should doubt that NASA has the capability to land a Roving Laboratory on Mars that will uncover most of the planets secrets, which rather forestalls the necessity for humans to travel to Mars.

COLONISING THE MOON IS ESSENTIAL TO SECURITY

What fascinates me Ronald is your paper in 2002 predicting the future for space travel and space exploration. I shall read to you the part of the story that I have cherished for the last ten years, because its predictions are so accurate. The Space Station on the Moon became a priority after scientists discovered that an Asteroid could hit the Earth in 2037. This is the story you recorded after a session of Visual Scrying, and is as relevant today as it was at the moment you recorded what you saw during your Visual Scrying, when you realised that colonising the Moon is strategically important to the security of Earth.

Our Moon is our nearest stable planet, and to prove the point American Astronauts have landed and set foot on the Moon, albeit for only a short time span.

Locked up at the Moon's Poles are billions of tons of water in the form of Ice. Such a large quantity of water makes it possible to build a self sufficient Space Station in a crater closest to the ice to aid protection from the extreme swings of temperatures on the Moon. Such a Station would be peopled permanently by Earth's Scientists and Astronauts.

The first essential; is to deliver an array of Super Solar Panels to a crater close to where the ice is located to provide a constant supply of heat and electricity. Ice would be loaded into portable expandable containers, and the heat delivered by the Super Solar Panels would melt the ice enabling the liquid water to cascade through pipes to drive a generator to provide an emergency standby source of electricity, should the solar supply from Super Solar Panels fail for some unforeseen reason.

When a reliable supply of water and electricity is established, it becomes possible to generate Oxygen from the water for earthlings to store and breath. The system would continue on to drive water through filters to take out the interstellar-bacteria that exist in space to provide clean drinking water that will be recycled to initiate food production. The final stage would be to use the Oxygen and Recycled Water to make material for refuelling Space Craft that would be landing at the Moon Space-Port, refuelling, and taking off after ferrying supplies of materials necessary for the running of the Moon Station.

A permanent self sufficient Space Station on the Moon would be bigger, much bigger than anything that could be built in space. The Moon is only around two hundred and forty thousand miles from Earth, and is still in mint condition. Furthermore the Moon's gravity is only one sixth of that of Earth, requiring a thrust level of only five thousand miles per hour to escape the Moon's gravity, making exploration of deep space a reality. A shuttle leaving Earth would be slowed by the Earth's gravity until it had travelled nine tenths of its journey to the Moon, when the Moon's weaker gravity would take over, assuring a soft landing.

This important Space Station would fulfil three very important functions. Firstly a base from which to launch First Strike Nuclear weapons to either destroy or deflect any Asteroid heading for planet Earth, secondly, ensuring that First Strike weapons are ready for use when a hostile Alien craft enters our solar system, and attempts to set up a Base on the dark side of the Moon, from which to plunder Planet Earth, and Thirdly, a Space-Port from which to launch Spacecraft into deep space, and a Space Port to where the craft can return, refuel and restock; transforming space travel forever.

Everything you have predicted did come about Ronald. We just had to wait for the Scientists to wake up to the realisation of the immense possibilities in your plan. To colonise and take control of the Moon before Aliens arrive.

ALIENS ARE COMING

I must ask you Sun Lin about your knowledge of Aliens? Modern Aliens Ronald, are not quite the images that which people expect to see, and I have a slight doubt about whether people on Earth are ready for such revelations, such as: All religions on Earth have a Sell-by date.

DNA is seeded across the universe by comets. On Earth the seeded DNA were imbibed by the most suitable primate. The first offsprings were born with the large brain, and the rest is history. However, only one of the humanoids survived to the present day. Comet seeding is not always good news, because Comets can distribute bacteria positively harmful to populations on Earth.

The large brain syndrome occurs on countless planets across the universe. Seeding was imbibed by as many different species as there are stars in the sky on rocky planets within the goldilocks zone from their sun, and held in stable orbits by the gravity of their moon systems, with air and water provided by local volcanoes.

Depending upon the strength of the gravity on the planet, the aliens may be squat and dumpy; birdlike with small arms and wings; all very intelligent, but not of an ideal a model structure and stature rendering them suitable for building and manufacture in the way that we understand. All these alien beings would look very strange to us earthlings.

CYBORG ALIENS ARE VERY DANGEROUS
AND MUST BE DESTROYED

On a serious note; there are very dangerous Aliens in the Universe, that are ninety five per cent Cyborg, and five percent humanlike, who barely remember the distant line to their human ancestors from their far distant past. These things have no ethics or morals in the sense that we understand, and plough through the Universe taking what they need, which will be human DNA and cells to refresh and revitalise their five percent human like parts, or animal parts and rare earths.

These Aliens are terrifying because they enjoy the use of spacecraft and telecommunication a billion years more advanced than anything we have developed. There is anecdotal evidence that Aliens have already landed Probes on Earth to take samples from animal and human species across the planet. Aliens will probably return to Earth as and when they choose, using communications and travel that we will not understand. What is certain is that no contact whatsoever should be made with Cyborg Aliens. Their craft must be destroyed on sight. This scenario alone is a prime reason for housing powerful Mandlebrot multi nuclear warheads on rockets stationed on the Moon. It is probable that Cyborg Aliens will use the configuration of the solar system in December 2012 to enter into our Solar system, and can be certain that we will be unaware of their entry, because their craft will be cloaked in a manner making them impossible to detect.

Keep listening and looking for Aliens and Alien Craft, but do not answer their calls unless and until we are confident that our governments can control them. You can be certain that nothing you have seen in your memory store will prepare you for the sight of an alien craft, or Cyborg Aliens. If governments see them first, we may never hear about it.

Cycling the Streets
The Sweet Potato Man.
Blessings Dear Brothers.
Enjoy this Feast
Of the Royal King!

A Woman was Asleep
On the Hard Ground.
Wooden Boards on her Feet,
Wooden Boards on her Hands,
Straw around her Body.

"Wake Up Grandma
Breakfast is served".

She Smiled,
We thought She was Dead.

Many are Found Dead,
Frozen to the Ground.
Never to Reach their Beloved Lhasa.

We Anointed her Hands and Feet
With Healing Oils.
Warmed her with Hot Butter Tea,
And lay her down with our
Warm Dung Fire.

We Prayed to Buddha
For her Safe Journey.

Dressed as my Ancestors,
Dagger at my side,
I Saddled my Horse
With my Golden Mandala.
Draped him in Prayer Flags.
Jingle Bells around his Neck.

As we make our way
To the Great Pasture Lands
Chomolungmo Greets Us
With a Blinding Stare.

Struck by Lightening
We lay Stretched out in Prayer,
The Monks burning the Sacred Incense,
My Heart Racing.

Now begins my Adventure
Here on this Sacred Ground
I will find my True Love.

The Future unfolds.
The Magic of my quest
Lies before me.
The Golden Footsteps
Lead me to Happiness
As the Beauty of the Day Begins.

Blessings to those
Who find this True Path.

Sylvia Gladys Rayner 2012

HOSTILE ALIENS
COULD USE THE MOON AS A BASE

It is important to colonise the Moon, because left unoccupied the Moon is the most likely place Aliens would choose to land and build a base from which to send Probes to Planet Earth. Aliens are extremely unlikely to use the Planet Mars for such a purpose, because Mars would prove to be impractical, whereas the Moon provides a three day window to enable an Alien craft to escape an attack by a Spacecraft sent from Earth. There is also sufficient empty land on the Moon over which to lay out large arrays of Aerials that would be needed to interfere with or fry all military communications on Earth before sending Probes to hide in Earth's Oceans.

Why Sun Lin, does travel through the Universe look so impossible for us earthlings in our slice of Time? So it is Ronald, although there are countless planets in the Universe brimming with life, only really advanced Cyborg nations succeeded on such a course.

The powers and intelligence of the Universe, in their wisdom, were aware that if habitable planets were in reach of each other there would be constant war, pillage, and trouble between them, as on Earth in the present time. The formation of the Universe, as it stands, renders that scenario impossible.

Very advanced Cyborg nations are travelling the Universe, Ronald. Ninety five percent robotic, they do not suffer the problems that would wipe out earthlings during such a journey. Planet Earth has a long way to go before being capable to undertake such journeys. It is far more likely that Cyborgs will appear in our Universe long before earthlings can undertake journeys beyond Mars manned by Astronauts.

I continue to find it extraordinary Ronald, that so many space enthusiasts continue to believe that an Interstellar Space Craft arriving in our section of the Universe will make its presence known for all to see, and risk being blown out of the sky by a nuclear tipped missile. If you were a Commander of such a Space Craft, a far more likely scenario is that the essential part of your plan would be to ensure that your presence, in what could be a very hostile planetary system, would be to avoid detection at all costs. This would be achieved by arriving with your Craft fully 'cloaked' on the dark side of the Moon. You would then feel secure in the knowledge from the intelligence gathered by your computers that it could take three days for a Space Craft from the habitable planet Earth to arrive into Moon orbit, where it would be easily destroyed together with any other intruding craft on what was now, Alien Controlled Moon. You would then be in a commanding position in which earthlings could do very little about removing you and your Space Craft. To the first to colonise the Moon goes the prize.

Your next step would be to explore planet Earth and Earthlings, using technically advanced Probes manned by robots. Any planet similar to planet Earth, but two to three billion years older, will have exhausted most of its natural resources, and seed material from which to manufacture essential resources. Aliens from such a planetary system would want to take samples of metal ores, rare earths, plant life, animals and animal reproductive systems, earthlings, and their reproductive systems, and so forth. Unfortunately, there is anecdotal evidence that this has already taken place across the planet.

I cannot stress sufficiently Ronald the importance of colonising the Moon; building a self-sufficient Space Station, and Space-Port housing powerful multi nuclear Mandlebrot weapons to defend Earth from asteroids and comets plus any unwelcome Alien Space Ships.

December two thousand and twelve is a time marker and wake up call for UFO watchers across the globe, particularly in the Americas, the Himalaya, and Scandinavia. Enthusiasts should dust off telescopes, and scan the skies during 2013. Groups should compare notes, particularly on probes suspected of diving into the seas and oceans where they can hide. Look for evidence of Alien presence and any location where Aliens may have visited planet Earth previously.

It is sad that you must now leave me Ronald, because someone greater than myself is waiting to speak with you to convey to you alone the most important message from Future Time that you will ever hear. The good news before you leave is that I have prepared for you the 'Book of Revelations 2013'. That work you found so troublesome Ronald. Your kind caring nature did not want to confirm the horrors ahead for mankind, and only I, Sun Lin your eternal friend and protector, could step in with a helping hand.

May the Powers of the Universe be with you Ronald; Go with my Blessing, and Protection!

Alien skull carved from phantom quartz
Revealing a map for alien contact

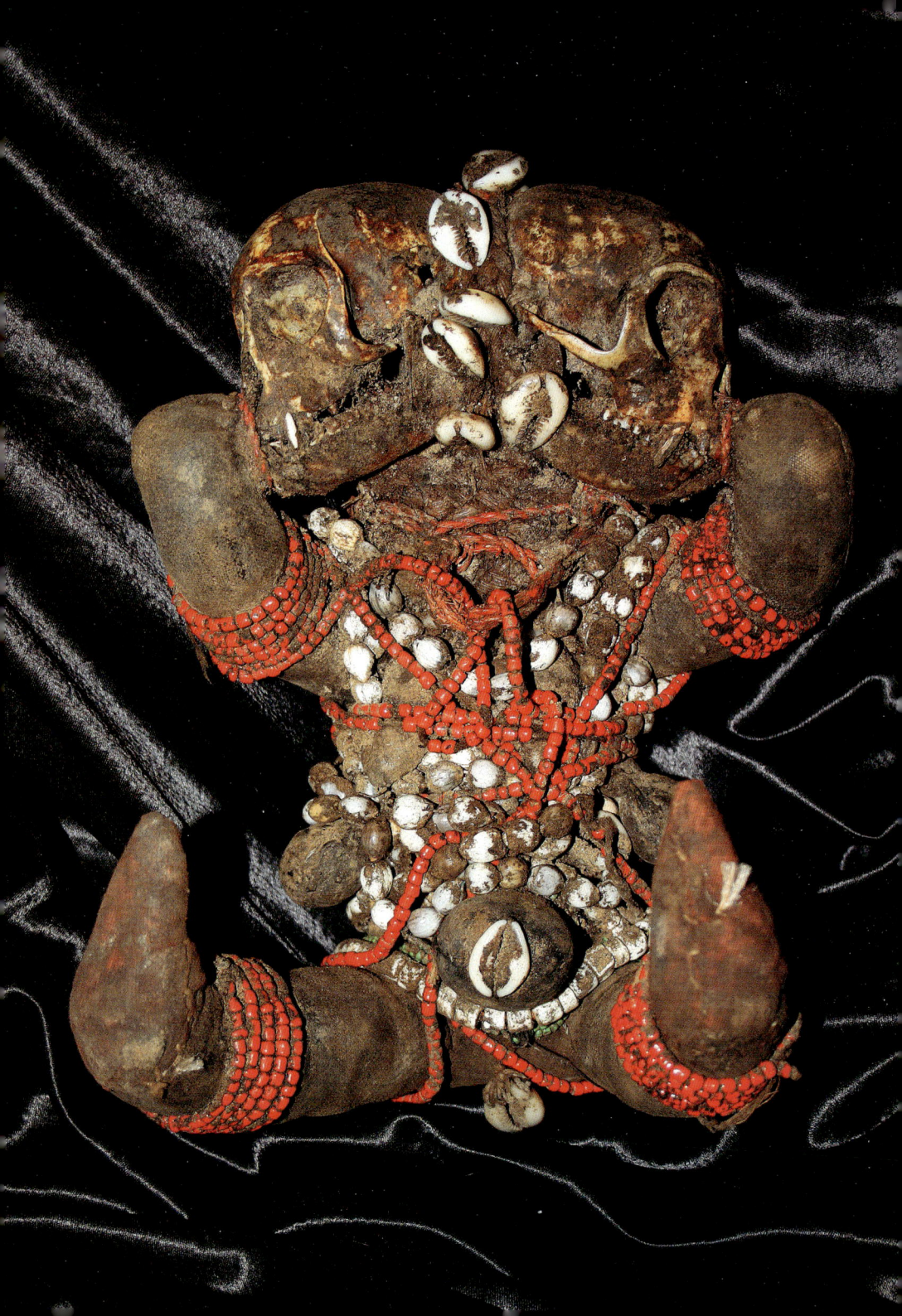

CHAPTER 53

NEW BOOK OF REVELATIONS December 2012

COMING DESTRUCTION OF CIVILISATION

New Destructive Life Threatening Weather Patterns Will Rule The Earth From December 2012 For 5,125 Years

Small but significant changes to the orbits of planets within our Solar system and Galaxy will have serious implications and consequences for weather systems across planet Earth. These changes will fetch new weather patterns that will rule from December 2012 for the next five thousand one hundred and twenty five years, outdating the systems, patterns and methods currently in use by Meteorological Offices across the world where Weather Forecasts are calculated.

Future severe Weather events, some of which are already upon us, plus Global Warming, will be driving destruction across the planet by increasing the number and severity and frequency of Earthquakes, Volcanic Eruptions, Tsunamis, Hurricanes, Floods, Droughts, Fires, and other severe erratic weather events such as Monsoons. Loss of crops will hit the US Economy.

Drought will become a regular feature across the American Midwest, where half of the world Corn is grown. Corn products and cattle production will fall by over fifty per cent in these areas affecting the livelihood of two thousand farms and millions of acres of normally productive farm land. Rivers will dry out necessitating a future relying on bore holes, depleting irreplaceable water sources. South America will benefit from exporting Corn to the United States and elsewhere in the world to make up the shortfall. The final result will be the doubling of food prices triggering unrest and rioting throughout vulnerable regions across the world. Over twenty million people through the Horn of Africa are in danger of malnutrition and starvation, which will become a long term problem.

Loss of fish stocks in parts of the Pacific Ocean, and the whole of the Indian Ocean will arrive by 2014. The warming of the oceans is killing off the phytoplankton on which fish stocks depend for their growth and survival, seriously endangering the survival of Island Communities and many mainland communities whose only source of food is the fish that they catch in the Ocean around them. The Crash of Fish Stocks throughout the Pacific Ocean and other oceans across the world is imminent, and will become apparent to governments within the next eighteen months to two years. It is already too late to remedy the problem in most areas. The 'Red Tide' of poison is coming.

Populations Will Crash
Some Megacities Will Be Abandoned By Their Residents
As In Mayan Times

Taken together, future events such as drinking water stress, and lack of sufficient food for a sustainable diet, will lead to population crash across several continents on a scale unprecedented in human history, overwhelming the best intentions of any government or Aid Agency. Drought and food stress will cause some Megacities to be abandoned, resulting in the deaths of millions of people, casting a question over the future survival of mankind in the effected areas. Over five hundred million people could die from disasters across the planet over the next few years.

Successive Indian Governments have failed to manage India's clean drinking water and Sewage, at a time when India's population is growing in numbers beyond India's ability to increase the supply of clean drinking water and sanitation necessary to meet growing demand. This explosive set of circumstances will lead to the eventual destruction on a large scale of the Country's population, preceded by unreliability of Electricity Supplies across wide areas of the Country, causing chaos.

There is a desperate need to increase the supply of clean drinking water to fast growing populations such as Mexico City for example.

Areas in the Middle East will increasingly come under water stress. Underground water upon which populations depend; water that is not replaceable, will run dry more quickly than anticipated. Growing water stress in the Middle East will lead to Skirmishes and Wars.

According To My Catastrophe Theory, European Countries Have Moved To The Tipping Point In History Where They Face 1,000 Years Of Economic Contraction and Decline

The European Union Will Slowly Fail In Its Present Form, Countries Will Default On Their Loans

For Europe, aside from the new severe arctic like weather patterns arriving in North America, Scotland, North of England, Northern Europe and Scandinavia, there will be one thousand years of economic contraction and decline effecting what history records were once ranked amongst the great Nations of the World. The Pendulum of long term growth has swung towards the prosperous emerging economies in the East. Even in the near term a dark cloud continues to hang over parts of the European Union, excluding Britain, Scandinavian countries, and the Russia's. This cloud will become darker during the intervening period leading up to the eventual disintegration and collapse of the European Union in its present form, where governments and banks continuing to play 'pass the parcel' and carry the Joker in the pack.

Against Stupidity – Even the Gods Fight in Vain

The Movements Of Planets Within Our Solar System Rule Everything, Including The Imminent Changes In The Cycles and Orbit Of The Sun

Traumatic events that I have predicted in my previous books enjoy a success rate of one hundred percent, and there are still many more catastrophic events waiting out there in Future Time. Most of the life changing situations waiting out there in Future Time are pre determined to a large extent by weather events triggered by the movement of the Planets within our Solar System, plus the effect of the rotation of our Solar System within the Galaxy. Added to which the cessation of the normal eleven year Sunspot Cycle during 2013/14, will usher in a three hundred year Solar Cycle during which the surface of the Sun becomes less active, fetching Mini Ice Ages to parts of the Planet in Future Time. There is a very close relationship between the formation and melting of Ice Ages and the activity of Earthquakes and Volcanic Eruptions across the Planet.

Everything that happens in the Solar System has a roll on effect on everything else. Following 2012, parts of the world could suffer many years of severe drought, while other parts of the planet will flood from too much rain falling in a compressed time period, triggered by the heating of the oceans.

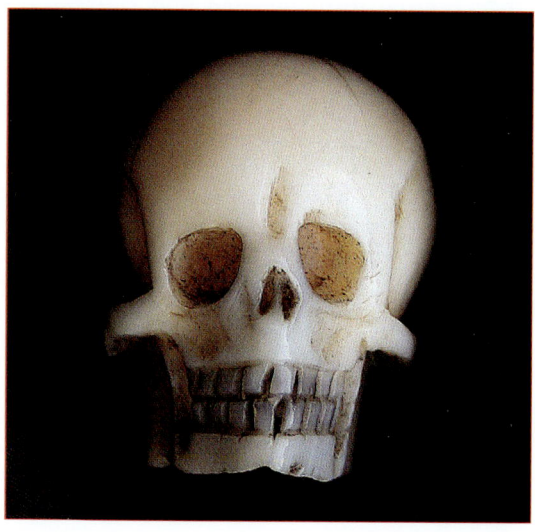

World Governments Are Not Warning The Peoples Of Planet Earth About The Dangers Ahead, Nor Are They Putting In Place The Measures Necessary To Ensure Survival Of At Least The Majority Of The Human Population

World Governments are not warning us about the dangers that are coming from Future Time, nor are they preparing the measures necessary to protect populations ahead of events. Meteorological Departments, Volcanologists, and Earthquake Scientists working in Universities around the world are generally underfunded. However, with the ugly face of Global Warming revealing itself, these Scientists should be given top priority for funding their research. Failure to do so will result in a clutter of pools of stale knowledge, leaving the public completely unaware of the dangers contained in the changed weather patterns that are arriving from Future Time.

CHAPTER 54

NEW BOOK OF REVELATIONS December 2012

THE EARTH WILL MOVE FURTHER FROM THE SUN

The Science behind my Predictions is an exploration of how patterns in mathematics run throughout the Solar System, and everything on planet Earth. It is all mathematics dear reader. It really is so. Whole weather systems move, fetching hundreds of years of drought and famine to new locations.

Our planet orbits the Sun, and as a Law of Thermodynamics dictates, the Sun being the larger body, gives off its heat to planet Earth, the smaller body. The sun is a massive star in comparison to planet Earth, but there is, nevertheless, an interaction to the loss of heat radiated to Earth and feedback particles radiate outwards towards the Sun from planet Earth.

A NEW SUN CYCLE IS IMMINENT

Every hundred thousand years the Earth is at its furthest distance from the Sun, the result is a reduction in the electromagnetic interaction between the two planets allowing the surface of the Sun to become calm, a phenomenon that reveals itself as a complete absence of the formation of Sun Spot activity on the surface of the Sun. The increased distance of the Sun from the orbit of Planet Earth, plus the absence of Sun Spot activity on the surface of the Sun, will result in less heat and UV rays reaching Earth. A new Maya Baktu cycle for the Sun is indicated to commence during December 2012.

THE INTERACTIVE CYCLES OF THE MOON

T he Moon orbits planet Earth. Planet Earth gives off radiated heat to the Moon in direct proportion to the distance of the Moon from planet Earth. The heat is radiated from the polar-regions on Earth, the Arctic and Antarctic, down to around forty degrees from each Pole. The Moon is also recorded in the Mayan Baktu Cycle.

When the Moon is closer in its orbit to planet Earth, the heat lost from both poles increases, allowing the ice caps and glaciers in both hemispheres to form, thus we see the start of an Ice Age. Conversely, when the Moon is further away from planet Earth, less heat is lost from the planet and a new warmer period commences. These changes relate directly to Earthquake and Volcanic activity across planet Earth.

THE END OF THE ICE AGE THAT STARTED 11,500 YEARS AGO IS IN SIGHT BUT A NEW SEVERE WINTER WEATHER EFFECT IS ARISING FOR NORTH AMERICA AND NORTHERN EUROPE

W hen the Moon moves further away from planet Earth by gradual movement to a higher orbit in its elliptical phase, coincident with the Sun running up to its 300 year cycles of becoming less active, less heat is radiated from, or lost from Planet Earths Polar regions towards the Moon. The result is that Polar Ice Caps and glaciers melt, pouring melt water into swollen rivers, and other melt water from rivers discharges into the seas. Thus begins the warming period, long before a Mini Ice Age arrives, due to shift in long term weather patterns.

One very important influence on the future weather for North America, Siberia and Northern Europe is the effect of the cold melt water pushing down upon and slowing the Atlantic Conveyor arising from the Caribbean. The effect will be to lower winter temperatures for the United Kingdom by as much as ten to fifteen degrees, which has various serious implications for Scotland, the American Economy, United Kingdom Economy and the Scandinavian Economies.

The Moon passes above and below the axis of Earth and Sun. One half of the orbital plane of the Moon lies below, and the other half of the orbital plane is above the axis of the Earth. THE ORBITAL PLANE OF PLANET EARTH IS NAMED THE 'ECLIPTIC'. At the changeover point the Moon is positioned exactly at the Ecliptic [when many Earthquakes and Volcanic Eruptions are triggered].

The points where the orbital planes of the Earth and the Moon interact are called the Lunar Nodes. Twice a month the Moon is positioned on one of the Nodes in the same plane as the Sun. A full revolution of the Nodes takes eighteen point six years, and produces a slight wobble of the Earth.

The Earth does not orbit the Sun in a circle, but an ellipse. The Perihelion describes the Earths closeness to the Sun. The Aphelion describes the position when the Earth is at its greatest distance from the Sun. When the Moon is nearest to Earth, we use the word Perigee, but when the Moon is at its greatest distance from Earth we use the word Apogee.

THE TRIGGER FOR A NEW ICE AGE IN THE FUTURE

The full rotation of the Earth on its journey through the Zodiac around the Sun takes about 21,000 years, causing the EARTH TO COOL, adding a trigger for a new Ice Age to begin; a phase within the cogs of the big unstoppable machine completely divorced from the effects of Global Warming.

At the time of writing the heated water in the Northern Pacific Ocean is driven by eddy currents towards the North Pole, where the heat is released into the atmosphere driving changes to the normal wind patterns of the Jet Stream, and allowing in Easterly winds from Siberia. The consequences of these changed wind patterns result in unusual and contradictory severe weather events to occur, such as the freezing of New York, London, North West England, and Scotland, overnight. At the extreme, people unprepared for the sudden freeze caught in the open would freeze to death before reaching home.

Archaeologists have uncovered clear evidence in past history of such events occurring across the planet. It is highly probable that the culprit will have been

Global Warming driving Easterly winds from Siberia to lower Latitudes. In the future all these events will occur in specific regions of the planet, whilst other areas continue to warm. At the time of writing this book, the frozen North is melting at its fastest rate for five thousand years and the Arctic ice melt has recently passed its 'tipping point'. And nothing can be done to prevent the continuation of this ice melt.

All these celestial phenomenon, are further complicated by the forty one thousand year cycle driving the tilt of the Earth, plus the twenty three thousand year cycle of Earth's wobble. Both phenomena are connected, and have an effect on Earth's weather systems.

WHAT GOVERNMENTS ARE
NOT TELLING THE PEOPLE

The Earth, Moon and Sun are obviously completely indifferent to the existence of humanity, but their movements at this period in the history of our Solar Cycle produces changes of infinite significance to the survival of the human race, much of which is not yet fully understood by Earth's scientists.

The 25,920 year cycle, the complete precession through all the signs of the Zodiac (to which I pointed in my last book) changes the mathematics of planetary interaction, and however small these changes, most changes have consequences for life on planet Earth, because the Earth reacts to the Sun in the same way that the Moon reacts to planet Earth, and there is the roll on effect of interactions with other planets orbiting within our Solar System.

One of the most important of these is the orbit of the planet Jupiter, a gas giant, whose travel varies slightly in its distance from the Sun. These changes, plus Jupiter's orbit, are responsible for the approximate eleven year cycle of Sun Spot Activity on the surface of the Sun, which has a direct bearing on the radiation of heat from the Sun striking planet Earth. At the close of each roughly eleven year Sun Spot cycle, changes in planet Jupiter's internal electromagnetism draw up heat from the Sun's centre to build sunspots, some of which will fire off as solar flares in the direction of planet Earth, disrupting satellites and power grids. In Future Time these regular Sun Spot Cycles will cease for a very long period with the subsequent roll effect on Earth's Weather.

A MINISCULE CHANGE IN EARTH'S ORBIT AROUND THE SUN WILL FETCH SEVERE ERRATIC WEATHER EVENTS IN FUTURE TIME

The natural orbits of the planets within our Solar System, and Galaxy, drive a one hundred thousand year Solar Sun cycle, and the lesser known three hundred year Solar Sun Cycle. Concealed within the latter is a reduction in radiated heat and UV rays hitting planet Earth for a period lasting one hundred and fifty years. This is due to the complete disappearance of Sun Spot activity. This loss of interaction between planet Earth and the Sun causes a reduction in electro magnetism across the surface of the Sun, and is directly responsible for a Mini Ice Age on planet Earth that will last for around one hundred and fifty years.

IN GREAT BRITAIN THE RIVER THAMES FROZE OVER

The first Frost Fair was held on the Thames in 1563, just below Westminster. There was a spectacular Frost Fair on the Thames in the seventeenth century that lasted a month. Oxon were roasted and Mulled Wine was sold together with Toffee Apples. The last Frost Fair was held in 1814.

During the one hundred thousand year cycle, the Sun moves further from or rather Earth's normal orbit is slightly further from the Sun, thus loosing the important electromagnetic interaction with Earth, plus the influence of Jupiter, which results in the surface of the Sun becoming less turbulent. Sun Spot activity on the surface of the Sun disappears altogether, and Earth loses its eleven year (approximately) Sun Spot Cycle. This event changes the rainfall pattern on Planet Earth which, according to my own theories, peaks over the last eighteen months of a Solar Maximum.

December 2012 marks the commencement of the eighteenth Sun Cycle, coincident with the close of the previous Mayan Baktu cycle that started in 3014 BC. A new Cycle begins on 23rd December 2012. [Note. all the planets in our Universe rotate around the sun].

CHAPTER 55

NEW BOOK OF REVELATIONS 2012

A WARNING FROM THE MAYAN BAKTU CYCLE

3014 BC TO 2012 AD

The Ancient Mayan Priests were Masters of articulating the Solar Calendar. Fifteen hundred years ago the Maya were able to plot the 26,000 year cycle of the Sun's orbit of the Pleiades. The Mayan great cycle of 25,627 years was divided into 5,125 year segments. The present great cycle ends on the 23rd of December 2012.

For me personally, December 23rd 2012 is very exciting because it fetches a new period in Earth's history alive by winding up of five thousand one hundred and twenty five years of Earth's past history in line with the Mayan Baktu Cycle. This cycle of history started around the time of Bronze Age Britain, and the disputed time of the great Prophet Moses in the Middle East. The Mayan Hieroglyphs talk about a time of flood, disaster and great changes taking place at the end of the cycle. All the evidence I have seen indicates that these events will be repeated in a similar way to those that occurred five thousand one hundred and twenty five years ago.

23rd DECEMBER 2012 MARKS THE BEGINNING OF 1000 YEARS OF LONG TERM ECONOMIC DECLINE FOR EUROPE

My Predictions for the years following on from December 2012 spell out the start of an Economic Winter that will permeate invisibly across the planet fetching economic contraction to the West; all part of my great 2000 year economic cycle of: One thousand years of economic development and progress that have now passed for Europe, followed by my

Catastrophes Cycle of one thousand years of economic decline and contraction for Europe which commenced in the year 2000, when my pen line fell off the edge of my graph, driving dark shadows across human consciousness in Europe. Writing now wearing my Mystics hat, this is a phenomenon that arises in the subconscious minds when populations are aware that something is changing; possibly to a situation that is bad for them personally, but their conscious minds are not aware of exactly what is wrong. This dark shadow will cause wide spread depression and an increase in Suicide rates across the world.

ONGOING GLOBAL WARMING FETCHES CONTINUOUS CHANGES TO WEATHER PATTERNS WHICH TOGETHER WITH THE RISE IN OCEAN TEMPERATURES ALREADY IN PLACE ON PLANET EARTH, WILL DRIVE ECONOMIC CRISIS THAT WILL BE ONGOING

Man made pollution basically stemming from over population is causing the oceans to heat up, particularly the largest bodies of water on the planet, the Pacific Ocean, Indian Ocean and Atlantic. The consequences are changes in weather patterns across the globe, triggering WIDE AREAS OF SERIOUS DROUGHT that will cause the death of millions. WATER STRESS due to the non availability of drinking water, and MASS STARVATION DUE TO CROP FAILURE AND LOSS OF LIVESTOCK TO DROUGHT CONDITIONS. SLOW SEALEVEL RISE AND FLOODS will kill millions (events that are already far advanced around the Horn of Africa).

Loss of plankton in the oceans and overfishing has already reduced fish stocks in many areas to a level from which they cannot recover, leading to starvation for many. The doubling of the number of serious HURRICANE EVENTS that could strike out to cover areas not previously reached. Tail ends of US Hurricanes will track across the Atlantic fetching high winds across Ireland, Wales, Midlands and North of the UK into Scotland.

SERIOUS INCREASE IN THE FREQUENCY OF VOLCANIC ERUPTIONS AND EARTHQUAKES

Extra weight of water from sea level rise weighing down on sea beds and the margins of Tectonic Plates, particularly along sea boundaries with land, will trigger EARTHQUAKES AND ZIG ZAG EARTHQUAKE STORMS REVERBERATING ALONG PLATE BOUNDARIES. New Zealand is a classic example. The heating up of the Pacific Ocean causing changes in electro magnetism that will excite magma, which is now happening under the Pacific and South America, driving magma to move across the planet in a way that will trigger MASSIVE VOLCANIC EXPLOSIONS DARKENING THE SKIES ACROSS PLANET EARTH. Many of the ice caps that have been weighing down upon and covering volcanoes in the past around Iceland, and holding the volcanoes in check for millennia have, in most cases, completely melted; Also in Siberia. Under Iceland lies one of the world's biggest shafts direct to the Magma Layer. YET ANOTHER PROBLEM PILED ON TOP OF THE subtle effect OF THE LONG COUNT MAJOR SOLAR CYCLE REACHING ITS MAXIMUM. There is nothing that can stop the inevitable fate for millions of people across planet Earth. These are events of a magnitude that are beyond government resources, because one massive earthquake event alone is sufficient to destroy nation and Island nations. The toppling of huge buildings in tightly populated areas will wipe away whole economies, together with many records. Neatly rowed residential buildings and commercial areas are replaced by carnage, pestilence, starvation and death.

ORIGINAL EARTHQUAKES

A Warmer World Means A Seismically More Active World Fetching Massive Earthquake Storms

A Warmer World results in the melting of Ice Caps and Glaciers across the planet, driving melt water into rivers and seas, causing sea levels to rise. Global Warming also results in the heating of the Oceans which expands the volume of water. The inevitable result is an increase in the volume and weight bearing down on ocean floors, pressuring tectonic plates, and the margins where oceans and plate meet the land. Anyone living on a plate boundary or in any Town or City close to where plates are colliding is always at risk. A classic example is New Zealand, where there is every indication in the upcoming seismically active world. Residents of New Zealand will remain at continuous risk, and is not a place to enter into old buildings in City Centres without being at constant risk of losing life and limb.

It is a fact that taken together, the effect of increased weight and additional water mass on ocean floors will increase seismic activity across surrounding Tectonic Plate boundaries, triggering Earthquakes and rock falls under oceans triggering Tsunamis. Two Earthquakes under the Indian Ocean off Sumatra off Indonesia, during the first half of April 2012 where lies the Indo Australian Tectonic Plate, did not result in a Tsunami because there were no rock falls or disturbance of sediment around the ocean floor.

REVERBERATING EARTHQUAKES

The two Earthquakes under the Indian Ocean in the first half of April 2012 could, in my own personal opinion, ('Original Earthquakes') reverberate stress transfer thousands of kilometres to drive an Earthquake Storm elsewhere. I use the words Earthquake Storm to reveal what can happen in a seismically active world, where Earthquake zones link together to produce a really massive Earthquake on a scale not seen for two and a half million years. It is my own personal opinion from my own calculations that the reverberations from the Earthquakes ('Original Earthquakes') could eventually drive through the North Pacific to produce a massive reaction in the San Andreas Fault off California, that will reverberate eight hundred kilometres from Ontario, Canada, down to California, and even drive to inland America between 2013 and 2018.

THE MOST DANGEROUS TECTONIC PLATE
ON THE PLANET
IS THE
INDO-AUSTRALIAN PLATE

The Indo Australian Plate is sandwiched between the African Plate on its left, and the Sunda Plate on its right, and is pushing upwards towards India. The subduction zone on its left running along the coast of Sumatra is a massive weak point. This plate will ride up and snap between the Northern most tip of Sumatra and the Southern tip of India.

NEW LAND BRIDGE, NEW OCEAN, DROWNING COUNTLESS MILLIONS, LAUNCHING THE MOST MASSIVE TSUNAMI EVER

When the Plate Snaps in two, the bottom half of the Plate will ride up creating a new Land Bridge between India and Sumatra, at the same time creating a new Ocean in the Bay of Bengal, and submerging Bangladesh drowning countless millions. The event will disturb all the other Tectonic Plates and launch the Highest Tsunami Ever that will race half way across the Globe.

SEA LEVEL RISE IS UPON US

BUILDING ON FLOOD PLAINS SHOULD BE STRICTLY PROHIBITED

The consequences of the beginning of sea level rise is little understood and ignored by most Planners, whereas it should be taken very seriously indeed and building on Flood Plains strictly prohibited. Not to do so will result in populations living in properties built on flood plains needing to be re-housed within the next ten to fifteen years.

Even very early stages of sea level rise have damaging effects on roads and properties bordering rivers and seas. Water seeps in and saturates ground, which means when it rains rainwater cannot drain away. Dampness starts arising in buildings fetching dangerous black fungus. Roadways start drifting and tarmac surfaces begin cracking and breaking up. At these stages there is no evidence of water lapping the front step. However, for those living close to rivers off estuaries, water starts lying around at high tide but never quite goes away. Not many years later these properties have to be abandoned.

CHANGES TAKING PLACE ON THE SURFACE OF THE SUN COULD AFFECT THE ONSET OF A MINI ICE AGE

During a session of Visual Scrying I saw the Sun in Future Time growing cooler, because there was a complete loss of Sun Spot activity on the surface of the Sun. This absence of Sun Spot activity is coincident with the exactitude of the Maya in constructing the cycles of the Long Count Calendar. Loss of Sun Spot activity indicates lower electromagnetism on the surface of the Sun. Normally as one Solar maximum ends, and a new cycle begins, Sun Spot activity appears on the surface of the sun and grows more active over the period of the solar cycle. Giant eruptions twist giving off Solar Flares, some firing out towards the northern polar region of planet Earth.

I saw no activity on the surface of the Sun in Future Time. This is a clear indication that the three hundred year solar cycle has arrived to trigger the one hundred a fifty year mini Ice Age. It is possible that this phenomenon will come along in time to prevent the Earth boiling over from manmade run-away temperature rise, but this will not save many areas on the planet.

Over time the surface of the Earth could also grow cooler as a result, triggering the one hundred and fifty year cooling of the planet.

The cycle of Solar Flares that are scheduled to peak in 2013 may be the last for a very long time in the new solar cycle when the Earth realigns with the centre of the Galaxy, and moves on to a one hundred thousand year cycle that takes the Sun further away from planet Earth. If Sun Spot activity ceases, some areas of the world will suffer one hundred years of continuous drought. Cities will be abandoned; some Societies will disintegrate. Extreme variable weather will strike areas in the North, such as the United Kingdom, rendering food production almost impossible. This will be followed by Mini Ice Ages, leading to unrest and war in affected areas.

WEATHER CONCLUSION

Weather forecasters confined to well tried and established systems will continue to be confounded as unannounced short spells of Arctic Weather events strike Scotland, and the North East of the planet, down to lower latitudes than in the past, striking across New York and America, driven by the warming of the Atlantic Oceans, opening the door to Easterlies to drive down from Siberia. Further Global Warming will roll on unabated in other parts of the planet, plus the tail end of Hurricanes from the North Atlantic driving in across Ireland and the West of England through to Scotland.

There will be unusually violent weather events with the doubling of the number of severe Category Five, Hurricanes originating off the Caribbean, one of which will turn right and work its way up the West coast of America to strike New York. My mathematics indicates that it is only a matter of time. Even when a Mini Ice Age strikes, driven by the new three hundred year Sun cycle, and loss of Sun Spots, Global Warming will continue unabated across other parts of the planet enveloped in carbon emissions. It is probable, however, that the cooling of the Sun will save the planet from the worst effects of Global Warming.

Think of the Universe as a set of moving cogs, all turning and causing other cogs to which they are linked to turn in a fixed pattern. Some cogs remaining tightly set in their grooves, until a gear change brought by elliptical orbits, when some of the cogs move out slightly from the tight setting but continue to turn all the same, in a simple relentless movement, winding through eventful cycles of around two and a half million years, one hundred and twenty six thousand years, and five thousand one hundred and twenty five cycles fetching Earthquakes, Ice Ages, Warm Periods, Sea Level Rise, Volcanic Eruptions, Tsunamis, and other disasters across the Globe. Events that Mankind is Powerless to Prevent.

VISUALISING GOD'S THINKING

It is not difficult to first picture in one's mind and then fully understand the way in which these terrestrial events continue in a never ending cycle across our Universe and Galaxy. Everything is locked together as in a giant machine, whose movements determine the fetching of Earth's Ice ages or warm periods, and influencing Earth's weather patterns, or possible meteor strikes. We know that because of the simplicity, beauty, and interconnectedness of all these phenomena, every part working together as one; it is like hearing God think. Only then can we know that every part of this pattern arises from very truth, and it is unfortunate that only Prophets can hear God Think.

It will be wise to come to the realisation that whilst the cogs and cycles are turning, 'WHAT WILL BE WILL BE'. In order to Survive, human kind will need to adjust to a new harsh impoverished hostile environment by improvising and adapting to conditions prevailing. No amount of prayer will stop the machine. However, the build up of good synchronicity through the way in which a person leads their life, prayerful thought, meditation, avoiding crime and sin, doing no harm to others, and understanding the importance of repenting any sins, will assure your survival.

God is the power and intelligence of the Universe. Man being so much lower than God, brings death and destruction upon the Earth and its inhabitants through over population and Global Warming, ruled over by pools of stale timeservers, and others whose behaviour is slowly returning to the animal from which they evolved. Is man, like the animals, a natural species for planet earth? All the evidence indicates otherwise.

How much longer will we have to suffer mankind? Not much longer if what I have seen through my Visual Scrying is any guide. It appears to me that The Powers of the Universe are preparing to Start Again.

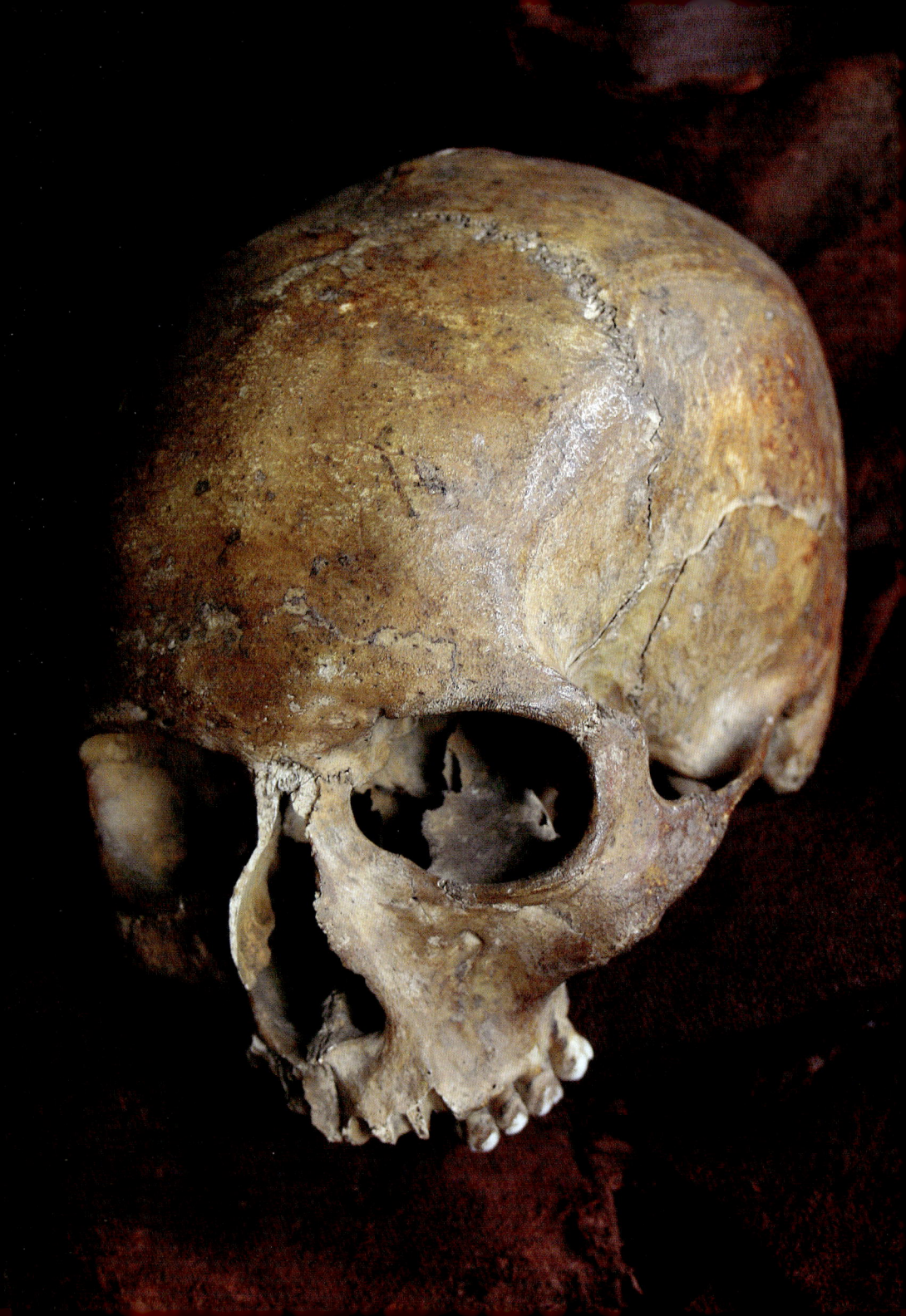

CHAPTER 56

NEW BOOK OF REVELATIONS December 2012
ARMAGEDDON WILL BE FULFILED
Food Catastrophe Is On Its Way

I am sad that you must leave me now Ronald, because someone greater than I is waiting for you with the most important messages you will ever hear.

Shortly after my farewells to Sun Lin I found myself moving through space as on a magic carpet, when I saw the **Skull of Doom** ahead of me, not striding across the planet as in His usual manner at past meetings, but standing with his feet planted firmly on either side of the Earth.

He called out with his booming voice, **Ronald my Prophet, blessed are you among all other men upon my planet. To those who tried to harm and revile you I have planted disease in their body and they will die slowly, giving them time to reflect upon their evil ways, and the unimaginable terrors they will face following their death. I will wait on them, and anyone who tries to harm you.**

It is My Will Ronald that you shall know the truth of all things. Hold your Crystal Skull above your head at midnight on the night of the Full Moon following the Autumn Equinox. You will see the Past and the Future touch, followed by a blinding flash, and for that moment you will become aware that you are fired with the knowledge of all things. When your eyes refocus, you alone will see a Future Time, revealing that when you wake up one morning in Future Time, the world will have changed in an instant. The past will have gone, and the things of man will have perished, but you my Prophet will be overwhelmed and uplifted by the great joy of just being alive.

I am now going to reveal to you alone Ronald my greatest secret never before told. I am going to rid the world of murderers, the violent, fornicators, the drunkards, the greedy, adulterers, and deceivers from this slice of time. **I will wipe away this filthy generation.**

I am going to rent the planet in two, using the greatest Earthquake in the history of Planet Earth. This Earthquake will raise the land and drive a great wave across the Oceans hundreds of metres in height, and travelling at great speed that will sweep away Islands and destroy major Cities.

Whole continents will move as a result of reverberating Earthquakes Zigzagging along Tectonic Plate boundaries. I am going to release this Great Armageddon that is long overdue.

Multitudes will suffer the Perdition that will come upon them as a thief in the night. Their mansions and precious stones, and fine living, plus their things of old stored up upon the Earth will depart from them. They will stand in rags reeking in fear and torment, weeping and gnashing their teeth seeing that everything they possess gained from the toil of others has turned to dust.

In one hour I will reap desolation across the planet, everything will be thrown down, and their riches shall be turned to ashes. Then I will follow with a short Ice Age that the survivors of this greatest of catastrophes may be reborn.

I will pass-over those who do not corrupt their bodies with drugs, fornication, drunkenness, violence, and greed, not using their lofty positions to gain pecuniary advantage for themselves only; not for the good of others. My chosen ones will wear my marks upon their clothes and above their doors. They will not be dripped in blood. They know who they are.

Great Cities, housing the vile drunkards, liars, cheats, adulterers, particularly those who deceive others to gain fine living for themselves. They will see everything they own on fire and despoiled. Only you my Prophet will know the time and the place of Armageddon, and those who come to you will be saved.

Oceans will disappear, but I will create an ocean where solid ground once stood. Rivers serving great nations will become polluted beyond imagination and many millions will perish. Then I will release my Plagues upon them. Sores and Puss will appear on the faces of the evil that survive in their rat holes. They will call out and long for death that will be slow in coming.

My Sun will dry up the lands of many great nations until they become ablaze. Many will perish watching their property and chattels destroyed before their very eyes.

Like the peoples of old in Sodom and Gomorrah, no man will believe that destruction will come upon them, because no man can be a Prophet in his own lands, but there is no escape. It is too late, the die for tomorrow is cast; Armageddon is waiting. The Revelations written by my Disciple St John will be fulfiled.

FOOD CATASTROPHE
SEE THE FUTURE OR DIE

A major shift in Earth's weather patterns predicted in my last book will fetch seven hundred years of drought to America's Grain and Cattle belts. Day time temperature will reach 105-115 degrees. The absence of rain will cause water sources to dry out, and there will be no moisture around. Pasture will be barren; there will be no soya, wheat or maize, or feed for cattle. Animal numbers will fall dramatically triggering unbelievable high meat prices never before seen to reverberate across the globe. Americas Mid-West will become a dust bowl. The shortages will be cumulative, year on year. A similar story will play out around the world, including suppliers such as Australia, and Eastern Europe. Unrest and riots will unleash across the globe. Millions will flood across borders in search of food. Food Aid will become non- existent.

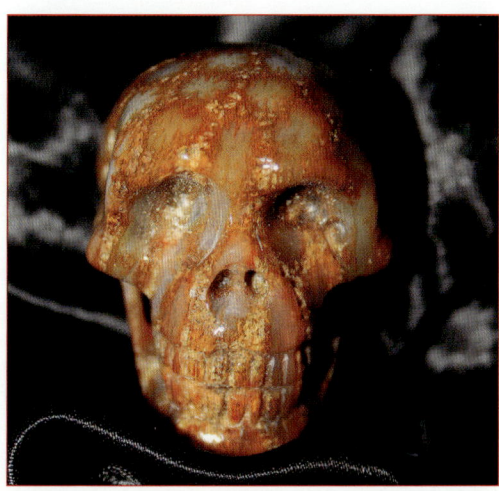

CHAPTER 57

MEDITATION

GAINING CONTROL OF ONES MIND

I have explained clearly the extreme Weather Events lying ahead in Future Time, followed by Armageddon. Most people in the world will ignore these warnings because it is not what they want to hear. To my faithful and loyal readers across the world I offer the following advice for dealing mentally with what they may experience in Future Time.

The brain records everything it sees and hears, laying it down like a record in the Subconscious mind. The Conscious Mind, your own personal Reality, will be completely aware that there is information recorded in the Subconscious. That said both the conscious mind and the subconscious mind are made up of layers, such as the deep subconscious. I believe there is sufficient evidence to state that both have invisible forces that extend beyond the body. One example is when we become aware that someone is staring at us, from behind. Another, perhaps not so simple an example is Mass Hysteria, and the Universal Collective Unconscious.

One way to access important bits of the record in the Subconscious and bring them into awareness is through Meditation. During Meditation the Conscious Mind is able to wander freely across the layers of information recorded in the Subconscious and draw them up into the Conscious Mind, which is the Reality playing out before you. It then becomes possible for the Conscious Mind to carry out the important process of working on puzzles or problems within the information, so that answers can drop into the Mind, sometimes during Meditation and or upon waking. Great scientific breakthroughs have arrived this way. Moments of insight are unpredictable, but meditation can make them less so.

A Mystic is someone who is adept at driving the parts of the Mind to work together in one's personal Reality. The Mystic also has the added ability of drawing upon information and knowledge from outside normal, from other equally valid Realities, information outside our slice of Time or beyond the leading edge of Time, not 'Now'. I refer to this phenomenon as the Evolutionary Leap. A Mystic in Meditation renders his mind without thought, but without the absence of thought; whose everyday thoughts are not on worldly things, but more developed above and beyond worldly things; understanding that truths and facts are one; that thoughts allowed to remain in the mind's eye can trigger unwanted emotion, and words held in the mind's eye can also trigger unwanted emotions.

Understanding how it is possible to gain control of the mind, through the understanding of the way in which it is possible to control the connection between the Subconscious Mind and Conscious Mind, and co-join them into one's normal Reality, makes it possible for individuals to move towards true enlightenment, gained from retraining the mind to become more intelligent in its operation.

Retraining the mind to work more efficiently creates something akin to the body's immune system. The mind becomes able to destroy or avoid thoughts or pictures coming into the mind that can effect and damage the healthy functions of the individual, either physically or mentally. By building an awareness of that which you dislike and constructing secret coordinates in the mind to ignore or reject the unwanted will ensure that a distorted Reality does not emerge.

These secrets were taught to me by Alien Monk, Sun Lin, as the only way I would become capable of coping with Visual Scrying. Avoiding fear, panic, feelings of insecurity and uncertainty – by not going there! Put simply, if you are watching television, listening to radio about disasters, something that might affect your livelihood – block out any thoughts of it applying to you personally or how you may feel in that situation – DON'T GO THERE.

Another way of explaining the theory is, for example, if you witness a serious road accident, do not imagine yourself in the position of the injured victim or close relative. Block out any thoughts – DON'T GO THERE [gives greater strength to deal with the situation].

In this way it is possible to avoid fears, phobias, feeling of insecurity or uncertainty, by the conscious realisation that the event does not apply or affect you personally. Nothing bad or uncomfortable applies to you. YOU ARE MERELY AN OBSERVER. Follow this course and it becomes possible to retrain the mind to rationalise thinking towards the realisation of the goal – YOU ARE ONLY AN OBSERVER.

Nothing worthwhile or rewarding comes easily, and so it is with my writing. I see evil as cold, hollow, a form of nothingness. I do not shy away from the unthinkable. I never allow desire to overtake reason, and anyone who does not find the middle way between desire and reason will never find peace. I look for the unexpected, fully aware that nothing will change unless one makes it change, whilst not ignoring death and the forces of darkness all around.

Start with Meditation and the realisation that the conscious mind can search the subconscious to discover every detail the brain has recorded; everything it sees and hears, and take it into the Minds Reality that plays out before you. Edit that information as it rises into awareness in the conscious mind by taking on the role of the OBSERVER, and not allowing fears or uncertainty into the subconscious where they may cause phobias or illness (these can often be removed by my theory of Structuralism, when the fear is drawn up into the conscious mind and then externalised into the physical world, and destroyed).

A clear and healthy outlook for your future starts with being the best you can be every day. Always leaving sufficient time to stop and stare at the beauty in nature all around.

I have demonstrated how you can take control of your Mind, and not allow your subconscious or conscious minds to take control of you before it enters the rational thought process. You will be able to look at manipulative advertising fired at you on television and see the content for what it really is. You will be able to discern the nasty, dishonest, deceitful people all around, for what they are, and avoid them. Always take care to do no harm to anyone. Do not join in conversation with people to talk sexual filth and adultery. Do not eat or drink to excess. A clean mind is a healthy mind a healthy mind drives good health and wellbeing into the body. Armageddon is coming. The Book of Revelations will be fulfiled, nevertheless; Always try to look on the Bright side of Life.

A SIMPLE EXERCISE IN MEDITATION

The practice of regular sessions of meditation will aid emotion and physical wellbeing, and reduce anxiety, stress, and aid mind function by bringing a racing mind into quiet. By concentrating everything on to mindfulness, mental and physical benefits will quickly accrue, and other improvements will follow, one improvement having a dramatic beneficial influence upon another.

My favourite position for meditation is to sit in a comfortable chair in my garden, or in my bedroom. I keep my spine upright and relaxed with my hands resting in my lap, having first loosened any tight clothing, as taught to me by a Tibetan Master. My personal preference is to start with the Lord's Prayer because it contains 'Power Words' used over a period of two thousand years. It is important to be warm and comfortable, and remain mentally positive; remember this is your time. After practice this position can be achieved even on a busy train or space. Sometimes I start by repeating mentally, OM MANI PADME HUM, gently pushing away any thoughts that come into the mind, so that the mind is blank. With my mind blank and remaining quiet and still, visions start to arrive, some in vivid technicolour. I keep them in my mind's eye and allow them to develop. When they disappear, I may drift off into a twenty minute sleep.

The immediate beneficial effects are a more relaxed and alert mind and body. The feel good factor will become noticeable after only a few days. This method has also reduced my blood pressure. Solutions to problems or good ideas may also drop into mind. Another method used is to be aware of and to count 'out breaths', dismissing thoughts that push into the mind. I prefer to use this latter method for light hypnosis to ease stress.

THE USE OF A TIBETAN MANDALA
FOR HEALING

The Tibetan Mandala is not an invention in art. The correct use of a Mandala is a method of exploring regions of our unconscious mind to discover that which we were not previously aware about ourselves; a practical way of looking below the conscious layer to reveal what has formed below the level of consciousness, and using Meditation to fetch the issues through to the surface. This is a process that can lead to the discovery of real self, usually revealing what a really good person we are inside.

Dreams are a mystery to most people, but intimate personal dreams can play a role in understanding the symmetry of the arrows pointing to the centre of oneself.

Meditating with a Mandala can relieve and liberate a person's phobias or mental illness; relief after a mental breakdown and depression by bringing tranquillity of Mind, Body, and Spirit. Tranquillity is another way of opening the door for what is lying in the unconscious mind, to get to the surface and renewing lost confidence.

In good times the patterns contained within the quadrants around the radials within the circle in a Mandala look ordered and attractive. At other times when trauma, for example, trigger complexes to split away from conscious mind, the symmetry is broken, revealed by an unclear and confused pattern; often a clue to an unhappy period of self. Taken as a whole, the pattern round a Mandala reveals the personality in its wholeness.

Any individual can set up their own personal Mandala, which is a tried and tested method of transferring hidden parts of our nature, and fetching them through to consciousness. If we discover that a phobia is revealed in the form of a spider, for example, one can make a paper-mache model; handle that model, and then calmly destroy the model. That Phobia will be gone!

If you are feeling down, repeat out loud. **Every day in every way I am feeling better and better, stronger and stronger, mentally stronger, physically stronger, and better in every way. Repeat every morning when you wake up**

and during every day for as long as it takes! Avoid people who take the proverbial and put you down. This exercise really will work, particularly for people who have lost their confidence.

Warning. Meditation is not a substitute for visiting a medical doctor when an ongoing illness is suspected.

THE SQUARE OF PEGASUS

The Horse Lay There
Sad Eyes
Trusting his Master.

The Boy kept Vigil
Through the Night.
Praying to the Blue Buddha.

Once More he took
The Old Sticky Yak Butter
Made a Ball
And Placed it Gently on to the
Painful Leg of his Friend.
As his Ancestors before him.

The Boy and the Horse
Slept Together.
Each Enjoying the Companionship
And Warmth.

Suddenly Awake
Full of Prayer and Wisdom
The Boy Raced Back to the Old Kettle.
Skimmed off the Green Slime
The Boy Smiles as it GLOWS
IN HIS HANDS.

SLEEP WELL MY FRIEND.

NOW THE MAGIC BEGINS.
THE MEDICINE BUDDHA
DOES HIS WORK.

Blown Above the Clouds
Into the Night Sky
To the Dream World of Healing.

Flying Easily with Beautiful White Wings.
Guided by the Hand of Buddha.
The Horse Enjoyed his Freedom
His Master Dreaming of
Thunderbolts and Zeus.

The BLUE MANDALA the TRUTH OF LIFE
Once again Shone like a Bright Star.

The Winged Horse Lost to Eternity
Waking from a Dream to the Morning Prayers.

The Soft Chanting Begins.
Joy in our Hearts.

The Secret of Life Unwinds
As the Heavens look down
Upon Us.

Sylvia Gladys Rayner 2012

The Great Prophet Moses
Painted by the Author Ronald Rayner

CHAPTER 58

The Sixth Sense, Precognition, Synchronicity, Entanglement

To understand Mysticism, the Sixth Sense and so on, it is important to grasp the fundamental difference between the Physical Body and the Mind. The body is a complex biological shell. The Mind is completely different. The Mind functions by electrical impulses across the brain. The Mind exists in its own Independent Reality

The Sixth Sense is explained as sensing something that is going to happen before it arrives. My research indicates that the Sixth Sense is very real; yet another hidden Field existing in the subconscious; that arrives in the Reality of one's conscious Mind. There are External Fields such as Universal Collective Unconscious and Synchronicity, Cosmic Consciousness, and Precognition. Some of these phenomena are able to extend outside the Mind, and beyond body; such as transference of thought from one mind to another and large scale shared emotion such as Mass Hysteria, whilst remaining in one's own Reality.

PREDICTING THE FUTURE

There is precedence in science that is almost certainly part of the same Fields – Entanglement. Here is an example – Entangle two Electrons. Place one entangled electron in the USA and its entangled partner in Russia; Repeatable scientific experiments have shown that whatever one does to one of the pair of entangled electrons, will occur instantaneously to the other entangled electron, faster than the speed of light. Two separate entangled Electrons at far distant locations from each other, experiencing the same interference simultaneously. My research points to the existence of an invisible Field/s in a Single Dimension; hidden Fields across the Universe in which conscious or subconscious thoughts or 'happening' travel across space, not confined by the physics of curved space time.

SCIENTIFIC CLUE TO SYNCHRONICITY

A Single Dimension – reveals to me a picture of an Horizon across the Plain to the edge of the Universe. The Horizon consists of infinite number of Field Lines containing information; Field Lines that can criss-cross to form an infinite number of patterns revealed in Synchronistic events reflected back as a Hologram of Reality. It would take more than the capacity of a single Super Computer, however, to calculate the number of patterns it is possible to create within a single dimension comprising crossed field lines.

It is obvious that the Information contained on the Field Lines or patterns travel faster than the speed of light because everything in the field travels in a straight line, whereas everything outside a single dimension is subject to the physics of Curved Space Time and Einstein's famous equation; everything that moves in curved space is subject to the physics of the speed of light. This proposition implies that Single Dimensions are not subject to Entropy (high or low entropy); whereas the adopted speed of light travels in a curve in three dimensional space time is subject to everything proceeding from order to disorder or chaos. It may be possible to find where these Single Dimension Fields are positioned by identifying particles travelling faster than the speed of light in a Collider.

THE IMPORTANCE OF DEVELOPING THE TECHNOLOGY FOR VIRTUAL PRECOGNITION OF CRIME IN FUTURE OF POLICING

D evelopments in technology will in future enable Police Forces across the United Kingdom to develop Computer Programmes capable of Precognition; enabling the identification of potential crime scenarios before the crime/s arise. Or the raising of Riots or any other potentially serious Public Order Offences. Burglaries, for example, can follow patterns. The technology exists to analyse the traffic and modes on Twitter, Face Book, Internet, Surveillance Cameras and Police Records, known familiar patterns of crime or public order events, and feeding all the information gathered into a Super Computer to achieve Virtual Precognition of Crime. Such an advanced system will enable senior Officers to make more accurate (forewarned) risk assessment in calculating the manpower and equipment needed for each situation before it is upon them, possibly saving resources.

Police Forces must be allocated funds additional to their existing budgets to enable them to take advantage of the Technological Renaissance that should be an automatic entitlement of the Metropolitan Police Force, and County Police Forces, to enable them to cope with the burden of reduced funds and officer numbers, at a time when Students and Criminals are fully aware that using the latest technology can spring surprises that could catch Police Forces unaware, or off guard, if the Police are in a position where they cannot better than match the latest development in technology available to the general public. Unfortunately it is always the Police who become the butt of government of public criticism, and not the lack of funding that restricts Police facilities, manpower, or equipment.

Perhaps the best way to raise the necessary funds for the installation of this essential superior technology, in a politically acceptable manner, is by attaching the costs of policing drunk and disorderly weekend revelry to the details of the crimes committed by each individual, and asking the Courts to pass these Costs down as part of the Sentence to the individual or individuals concerned, and returning the costs recovered to the police force involved. Not only will the money equip Police with the means of advance intelligence that is essential to policing the future, it will discourage irresponsible behaviour by hooligans and louts, because repeated lawbreaking will be a very costly adventure from which they cannot escape, because the offenders sentence will not be extinguished until a fine handed down with a sentence is paid in full.

VIRTUAL REALITY COMPUTER PROGRAMME WILL PROVIDE PRECOGNITION OF CRIME

Every thinking person respects the Metropolitan Police, particularly for their success in policing the London Olympics in 2012, I am confident that no taxpayer would begrudge extra funding to develop the latest technology to enable police to set up a Precognition of Crime Computer using Virtual Reality. In my opinion this development is important for the Future of Policing. In all other issues the Metropolitan Police have the upper hand, and could certainly teach the Police in America how to fetch a closure to 'Occupy' movements without the use of tactics that can drive the future leaders of the country to dislike or mistrust the police. Resentment against the police never arose in London, following on from action by London's Metropolitan Police to gain control of occupied areas.

I live in a small Essex village, and I can report with confidence that Essex Police are one of the finest rural forces in the United Kingdom, but I feel confident that all County Police Forces could benefit from information fed down from a Scotland Yard Virtual Reality Super Computer; programmed to link Forces closer together, and extended to Courts, to save officers time attending Court Hearings, other than appearing on video screen links. How else would Police Forces across the UK cope if the Government introduced a Poll Tax, for example! A Tax levied per head of adult population.

LIFE AND DEATH IS VERY REAL

My research indicates that the Mysterious Fields that I have uncovered in my research will go a long way to explaining my theories on Life After Death. Animals have a Soul, human kind have a Spirit. Both are part of the Life Force that permeates the Universe guaranteeing that life will arise even in its simplest forms everywhere on any planet where conditions for life exist, starting with extreme-o-files.

In human kind, after death, the layers in the conscious mind and subconscious mind, containing the Reality of the Mind; memories from every minute of every day, including thoughts, leave the body at the instant of brain death, moving through the Life Force Field in an instant from emitter to destination. The laws governing the Universe dictate that the Life Force can only move forward into Future Time with the Arrow of Time.

This same Life Force Field triggered by elements in the body determines the point of Brain Death. If death is premature, the Life Force leaves the body in the twinkling of an eye, moving onwards into the Future. After the point of death when the Spirit leaves the physical body, and moves into Future Time in the blink of an eye, Spirit ceases to be aware of past, or any means or way of contacting past. Life after Death requires only the existence of an Intelligent Universe, the proof of which is that we are here and now.

At a time that is fast growing into a Post Religious period in world history, where there is a growing realisation that the Ten Commandments, essential to the survival of a humane society can be got or won by altruism, it is comforting to know that without Human Consciousness the Universe would be unable to see itself or be aware of its existence – which is the whole purpose of human existence, and for this reason alone, our Intelligent Universe is not going to allow even one Human Spirit to be destroyed, save for those that have returned to the animal and serve no purpose for continuing in the Universe. It is also comforting to know that personal prayer, repentance, being the best we can be every day; doing harm to no one and keeping the Commandments is vital to altruism towards the continuation of our own Spirit after death. If you however are a DEVIL, repent and change for;

BEWARE OF THE ARMAGEDDON THAT IS COMING

FOR IT MAY BE COMING FOR YOU

and your Spirit will be

Wiped Away Forever!

In the Land of Mystery
Where the Shaggy Yak Dwells
Where the Great Eagles Fly
They Found my Brother

In his Hand the Book of a Hundred Names
A Gift from our Ancestors.

HE WAS DEAD

His Prayer Wheel, Flags and Bells with him.

The YAK was FEARLESS
As they Swam the Frozen Waters
Deep was the Snow.
They were Lost Forever in Time and Space
Never to Return to Me.

As I Lay by that River
The Stars shine down Upon Me
His Face Appears

I feel his Arms around me
And the Warmth of his KISS OF LIFE

The Wonders of the World before me
And nothing to Seek but the Future.

I Touch his Hand
And Ignite into a FLAME

The Joy of his Life Surrounds Me
And the Laughter of the
Child never leaves me.

There is always LIFE
There is always DEATH
There is always HOPE

OM MANI PADME HUM

Sylvia Gladys Rayner 2012

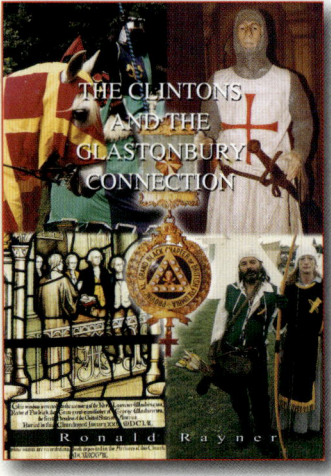

Amazon Kindle

www.
josephofavalon
.com

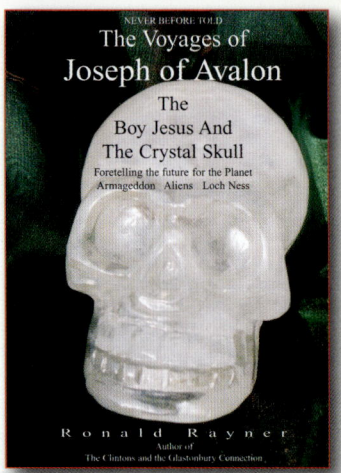

ISBN 978-0-9557906-1-4

www.
josephescapes
.com

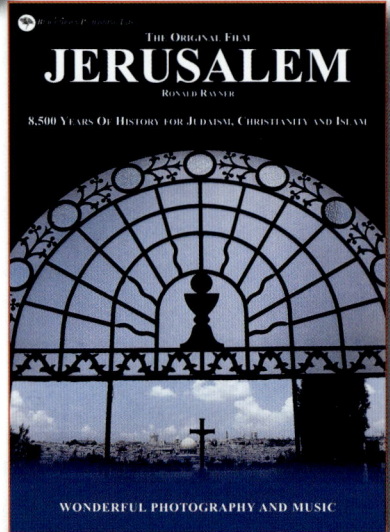

www.
alienmonk
.com

DVD 5-060172460007

ISBN 978-0-9557906-2-1

www.
jesusincornwall
.com

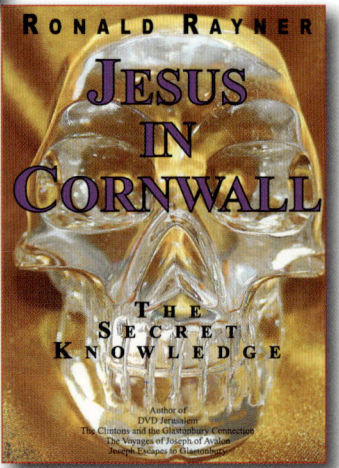

ISBN 978-0-9557906-3-8